FINALLY COMES THE POET

FORTRESS PRESS BOOKS
BY WALTER BRUEGGEMANN

The Land: Place as Gift, Promise, and Challenge in the Biblical Faith (1977)

The Prophetic Imagination (1978)

The Creative Word: Canon as a Model for Biblical Education (1982)

David's Truth in Israel's Imagination and Memory (1985)

Hopeful Imagination: Prophetic Voices in Exile (1986)

Israel's Praise: Doxology against Idolatry and Ideology (1988)

Finally Comes the Poet: Daring Speech for Proclamation (1989)

Interpretation and Obedience: From Faithful Reading to Faithful Living (1991)

Old Testament Theology: Essays on Structure, Theme, and Text (1992)

Texts under Negotiation: The Bible and Postmodern Imagination (1993)

A Social Reading of the Old Testament: Prophetic Approaches to Israel's Communal Life (1994)

The Psalms and the Life of Faith (1995)

The Threat of Life: Sermons on Pain, Power, and Weakness (1996)

Finally Comes the Poet

DARING SPEECH FOR PROCLAMATION

Walter Brueggemann

FORTRESS PRESS   MINNEAPOLIS

FINALLY COMES THE POET
Daring Speech for Proclamation

Cover design by Terry Dugan.

Library of Congress Cataloging-in-Publication Data

Brueggemann, Walter.
    Finally comes the poet : daring speech for proclamation / Walter
Brueggemann.
        p.   cm.
    Includes bibliographies.
    ISBN 0-8006-2394-0
    1. Preaching.   2. Bible—Language, style.   I. Title
    BV4211.2.B75   1989
    251—dc20   89-37524
                                                                      CIP

The paper used in this publication meets the minimum requirements of American National Standard for Information Sciences—Permanence of Paper for
Printed Library Materials, ANSI Z329.48-1984.   (∞)™

Manufactured in the U.S.A.   AF 1-2394

98   97   96   5   6   7   8   9   10

FOR
Lisa
Jim
John

Contents

After the seas are all cross'd, (as they seem already
    cross'd,)
After the great captains and engineers have accomplish'd
    their work,
After the noble inventors, after the scientists, the chemist,
    the geologist, ethnologist,
Finally shall come the poet worthy of that name,
The true son of God shall come singing his songs.

Walt Whitman, Leaves of Grass

Preface

This manuscript was prepared and presented as the 1989 Lyman Beecher Lectures at Yale Divinity School. The Beecher Lectures are by definition addressed to the subject of preaching. In these lectures, I have sought to address the crisis of interpretation the preacher faces in our culture, which has either dismissed or controlled the text. Preaching as an act of interpretation is in our time demanding, daring, and dangerous.

That crisis in interpretation is matched by a crisis of categories in scripture study that greatly compounds the problem of preaching. It is increasingly clear that what the text "means" for us is not simply a matter of exegesis, but concerns the large ideological realities in our society that rob us of our capacity to speak, our capacity to care, and our capacity to notice. Preaching and interpretation, however, exist precisely for such situations. It is the task of preaching to provide a ground and energy for speech, care, and notice. As we seek new modes of speech appropriate to our situation of interpretation, we shall find them, I suggest, exactly in the texts whose modes of speech we have mostly ignored. My book is an act of gratitude to that host of preachers who regularly exercise daring and danger in their act of preaching.

In presenting the Beecher Lectures, I was graciously and generously hosted by Dean Leander E. Keck and Professor Brevard S. Childs, and I am grateful to them. Subsequent to the Beecher Lectures, portions of this book were also presented as the Gray Lectures at Duke Divinity School, the Sizemore Lectures at Midwestern Baptist Theological Seminary, and Ministers Convocation at the School of Theology at Claremont. I am, as always, grateful to John A. Hollar for his meticulous care and steadfastness as my editor who relentlessly makes sense of my inchoateness. I am grateful to Gayle Medlin who has persevered in typing and retyping.

I am pleased to dedicate this book to my children who live always at the edge of poetic possibility, even in the face of my severe prose.

Walter Brueggemann
Columbia Theological Seminary
May 12, 1989

Introduction

Poetry in a Prose-Flattened World

A Truth Greatly Reduced

The preacher in U.S. culture deals with a claim that is commonly accepted as the truth by the listeners.[1] That is, we preach mostly to believers. There is a casual, indifferent readiness, even in our increasingly secularized society, to grant the main claims of the gospel—not to grant them importance, but to accept them as premises of religious life. In fact it is precisely the problem for the proclamation of the gospel that the great claims of the gospel do not seem to be problematic or in question.

The gospel is too readily heard and taken for granted, as though it contained no unsettling news and no unwelcome threat. What began as news in the gospel is easily assumed, slotted, and conveniently dismissed. We depart having heard, but without noticing the urge to transformation that is not readily compatible with our comfortable believing that asks little and receives less.

The gospel is thus a truth widely held, but a truth greatly reduced. It is a truth that has been flattened, trivialized, and rendered inane. Partly, the gospel is simply an old habit among us, neither valued nor questioned. But more than that, our technical way of thinking

1

reduces mystery to problem, transforms assurance into certitude, revises quality into quantity, and so takes the categories of biblical faith and represents them in manageable shapes.[2]

Or, if our technical reason does not pervert the truth of the gospel in relative naivete, our unwitting embrace of social ideology distorts the news so that it can be accommodated to a variety of social ideologies, of the right and of the left.[3] While my propensities are to value more greatly ideologies of the left, any ideology—by which I mean closed, managed, useful truth—destroys the power and claim of the gospel. When we embrace ideology uncritically, it is assumed that the Bible squares easily with capitalist ideology, or narcissistic psychology, or revolutionary politics, or conformist morality, or romantic liberalism.[4] There is then no danger, no energy, no possibility, no opening for newness!

Preaching among us happens in this context in which truth is greatly reduced. That means the gospel may have been twisted, pressed, tailored, and gerrymandered until it is comfortable with technological reason that leaves us unbothered, and with ideology that leaves us with uncriticized absolutes. When truth is mediated in such positivistic, ideological, and therefore partisan ways, humaneness wavers, the prospect for humanness, is at risk, and unchecked brutality makes its appearance.[5] We shall not be the community we hope to be if our primary communications are in modes of utilitarian technology and managed, conformed values.[6] The issues facing the church and its preachers may be put this way: Is there another way to speak? Is there another voice to be voiced? Is there an alternative universe of discourse to be practiced that will struggle with the truth in ways unreduced?[7] In the sermon—and in the life of the church, more generally, I propose—we are to practice another way of communication that makes another shaping of life possible; unembarrassed about another rationality, not anxious about accommodating the reason of this age.[8]

The task and possibility of preaching is to open out the good news of the gospel with alternative modes of speech—speech that is dramatic, artistic, capable of inviting persons to join in another conversation, free of the reason of technique, unencumbered by ontologies that grow abstract, unembarrassed about concreteness. Such speech, when heard in freedom, assaults imagination and pushes out the presumed world in which most of us are trapped. Reduced speech leads to reduced lives. Sunday morning is the practice of a counter life through counter speech. The church on Sunday morning, or whenever it engages in its odd speech, may be the last place left in our society for imaginative speech that permits people to enter into new worlds of faith and to participate in joyous, obedient life.

A Subversive Fiction

To address the issue of a truth greatly reduced requires us to be *poets that speak against a prose world.* The terms of that phrase are readily misunderstood. By prose I refer to a world that is organized in settled formulae, so that even pastoral prayers and love letters sound like memos. By poetry, I do not mean rhyme, rhythm, or meter, but language that moves like Bob Gibson's fast ball, that jumps at the right moment, that breaks open old worlds with surprise, abrasion, and pace. Poetic speech is the only proclamation worth doing in a situation of reductionism, the only proclamation, I submit, that is worthy of the name *preaching.* Such preaching is not moral instruction or problem solving or doctrinal clarification. It is not good advice, nor is it romantic caressing, nor is it a soothing good humor.

It is, rather, the ready, steady, surprising proposal that the real world in which God invites us to live is not the one made available by the rulers of this age. The preacher has an awesome opportunity to offer an evangelical world: an existence shaped by the news of the gospel.[9] This offer requires special care for words, because the baptized community awaits speech in order to be a faithful people. What a way to think about a poetic occasion that moves powerfully to expose the prose reductions around us as false!

The tensive interface between a reduced world of prose and a poetic speech of vitality requires us to consider the peculiar role of dramatic, poetic communication, the very kind given us in the text of the Bible. Such speech may seem odd and superfluous among us in our technological inclination. The case is made by many voices, however, that such speech that is daring, liberated, and unaccommodating is crucial, if we are to maintain a possibility of genuine humaneness.

Because we live so close to the biblical text, we often fail to note its generative power to summon and evoke new life. Broadly construed, the language of the biblical text is prophetic: it anticipates and summons realities that live beyond the conventions of our day-to-day, take-for-granted world. The Bible is our firm guarantee that in a world of technological naivete and ideological reductionism, prophetic construals of another world are still possible, still worth doing, still longingly received by those who live at the edge of despair, resignation, and conformity. Our preferred language is to call such speech prophetic, but we might also term it poetic.[10] Those whom the ancient Israelites called prophets, the equally ancient Greeks called poets. The poet/prophet is a voice that shatters settled reality and evokes new possibility in the listening assembly. Preaching continues that dangerous, indispensable habit of speech. The poetic speech of text and of sermon is a prophetic construal of a world beyond the one taken for granted.

Hans Urs von Balthasar, the magisterial Roman Catholic scholar, has written of this shattering, evoking speech:

> God needs prophets in order to make himself known, and all prophets are necessarily artistic. What a prophet has to say can never be said in prose.[11]

This poetic/prophetic utterance runs great risk. It runs the risk of being heard as fantasy and falsehood.

Indeed, judged by the firm, settled, technical certitude of this age, or measured by the uncritical ideology of the world we take for granted, the world offered in the biblical tradition of poetic utterance hardly has a claim to reality. It so little fits with the presumed world around us that the evangelical world of the tradition sounds like fiction. The notion of fiction, however, is not so precarious or easily dismissed as we might imagine. It is precisely the daring work of fiction to probe beyond settled truth and to walk to the edge of alternatives not yet available to us. It is this probe behind our settlements that makes newness possible. The more tightly we hold to settled reality, the more likely the alternative construal of the poet will be dismissed as "mere fiction." The poet/prophet, however, does not flinch from "fiction," for the alternative envisioned in such speech is a proposal that destabilizes all our settled "facts," and opens the way for transformation and the gift of newness.

In meditating on the daring of poetic speech to move beyond settled reality, Wallace Stevens does not flinch from using the category of fiction. Impossibly daring visions of the possible are the prerequisite to move beyond the truth so long held that it kills. Stevens writes,

> It is possible, possible, possible. It must
> Be possible. It must be that in time
> The real will from its crude compoundings come,
>
> Seeming, at first, a beast disgorged, unlike,
> Warmed by a desperate milk. To find the real,
> To be stripped of every fiction except one,
>
> The fiction of an absolute . . . .[12]

Garrett Green concludes his essay honoring Hans Frei with these suggestive words:

> The important point to be emphasized, to theologians especially, is that this story, however enigmatic, is the true story, the only story Christians have to tell,

and that it has no unstoried form. If it sometimes
seems so incredible as to strain the imagination and
offend the reason, the wise theologians will attempt
no defense beyond a reminder (paraphrasing 1 Cor.
1:25) that the fictions of God are truer than the facts
of men.[13]

The entertainment of a "fiction" drives us beyond known
truth. From the great narratives of Israel to the prophetic
poems to the testimony of early Christians, the singers
and storytellers spoke dangerously about dangerous matters, about new possibilities. The settled, entrenched, and
certain heard only fiction, but it was a "fiction" more powerful than facts.

In this book, then, I want to consider preaching as
a poetic construal of an alternative world. The purpose of
such preaching is to cherish the truth, to open the truth
from its pervasive reductionism in our society, to break
the fearful rationality that keeps the news from being new.
In framing this theme, I have borrowed a phrase from
Walt Whitman who celebrates the cruciality of poetry. To
be sure, Whitman intends something other than I intend.
Nonetheless, his words say well what I think we must
struggle with:

> After the seas are all cross'd,
>   (as they seem already cross'd,)
> After the great captains and engineers have
>   accomplish'd their work,
> After the noble inventors, after the scientists,
>   the chemist, the geologist, ethnologist,
> Finally shall come the poet worthy that name,
> The true son of God shall come singing his songs.[14]

After the engineers, inventors, and scientists, after all such
control through knowledge, "finally comes the poet." The
poet does not come to have a say until the human community has engaged in its best management. Then perchance
comes the power of poetry—shattering, evocative speech
that breaks fixed conclusions and presses us always toward
new, dangerous, imaginative possibilities.[15]

I shall argue that the continuing practice of this artistic speech voiced in the prophetic construal of the Bible is the primary trust of the church and its preaching. This speech prevents our reduced world from becoming brutal and coldly closed upon us. This speech, entrusted to and practiced by the church, is an act of relentless hope; an argument against the ideological closing of life we unwittingly embrace.[16]

A New World Voiced

The meeting of the community of faith is a speech meeting. We gather for speaking and listening of an odd kind. That meeting has the potential of evoking a new humanity. There are four partners who need to be present in the meeting so that the new reality can be birthed.

1. The first partner in the meeting is *the text.* The congregation gathers with a vague memory of the text—a memory that has the text mostly reduced, trivialized, and domesticated. It has been necessary to reduce the text all week, because there is neither time nor freedom for nuance, and because reductionism may permit one a tenacious hold on just a hint of the claim of the text. The community does not doubt the text, but it has been mostly impossible to remember the text all week with its angular scandal, its tensiveness, its density, and its amazement. All week we have been practicing our nervy autonomy where God is not real. All week we have been watching Dan Rather with little news items, and we become dulled to the real news that mocks the world of Dan Rather and dismisses the comments of Paul Harvey. All week the ideology of our nation, our class, our sect, our sex has seemed closed, settled, and ready for defense. We trust excessively and vigorously in our ideological commitments, which we accept as a rendering of the text. In such excessive trust, we do not venture beyond the little commitments of our ideology to face the troubled mysteries of life. We reason, in our uneasy confidence, that it is better

to have even a modest resolution than none at all. Without our little ideological resolutions, the realities around us are too wild and unsettled. So we cling to the biblical text, now domesticated by our tenacious ideology. The text lingers in our midst, but it has been misshapen and diminished, and robbed of its dangerous power.

In its distorted voice, the text has come to sound strangely like Adam Smith or Thomas Hobbes or Jacque Rousseau or Alfred North Whitehead or Karl Marx or Carl Jung or Eric Berne or Daniel Moynahan. There is then a wistful wonderment when we gather again around the text on Sunday morning. What is that text into which I have been baptized? Is there a life carried in the text? Is there indeed a word from the Lord that would let me live? The answer in part depends on this: Is there a poet who can render the text clearly without fuzziness, but also without a seducing certitude that covers over where I live? Is there a word there that can rescue me from my exhausted coping?

2. The second partner in the meeting is *the baptized*. The community gathers to be shaped by a text that addresses us, an articulation of reality that lies outside of us that we cannot conjure and need not defend. The ones who gather have been baptized. They may understand only in an inchoate way, but they have in fact made some vague decision about the cruciality of this text. They do not have a clear articulation of the text's authority. Or they have a clear articulation that has become so scholastic as to be without use. Nonetheless, they are prepared to accept, in a general way, that this text is their text, the voice of life addressed to them.[17]

The baptized, then, have been struggling with this text. The ones gathered are those who have either been trying other texts and have found them wanting, or have greatly resisted other texts and need this text reiterated once again. Either way, out of compromise or resistance, the community gathers not for entertainment or private opinion, or even for problem solving, but for the text made available yet again. They gather to hear the text that is shamelessly theological, candidly kerygmatic, and naively eschatological. The community waits for the text that may be a tent for the spirit. It waits with the hopeful yearning that the "house of authority" is still intact.[18] But if the text is to claim authority it will require neither the close reasoning of a canon lawyer, nor the precision of a technician, but it will require an artist to render the text in quite fresh ways, so that the text breaks life open among the baptized as it never has before.

3. There is a text in its boldness. There is a congregation, perhaps reduced and diminished by fatigue. Third, there is *this specific occasion* for speech. When the music stops and the rheostat is turned down, then there is this precious, awesome moment of speech. It is not time for cleverness or novelty. It is not time for advice or scolding or urging, because the text is not any problem-solving answer or a flat, ideological agent that can bring resolve. This moment of speech is a poetic rendering in a community that has come all too often to expect nothing but prose. It is a prose world for all those who must meet payrolls and grade papers and pump gas and fly planes. When the text, too, has been reduced to prose, life becomes so prosaic that there is a dread dullness that besets the human spirit. We become mindless conformists or angry protesters, and there is no health in us. We become so beaten by prose that only poetic articulation has a chance to let us live.

Into this situation, in this moment, the preacher must speak. She does not get to speak a new text. She must speak an old text—the one everybody knows. From the very first syllable, the ending is already known. But it is a script to be played afresh, so that in this moment of drama the players render the play as a surprise to permit a fresh hearing, a second opinion. It is an artistic moment in which the words are concrete but open, close to our life but moving out to new angles of reality. At the end, there is a breathless waiting: stunned, not sure we have reached

the end. Then there is a powerful sense that a world has
been rendered in which I may live, a world that is truly
home but from which I have been alienated.[19] The speaker
must truly be a poet. After the scientist and the engineer,
"finally comes the poet" (which Israel calls prophet)—to
evoke a different world, a new song, a fresh move, a new
identity, a resolve about ethics, a being at home.

4. There is a text that looms in resilient power.
There is a waiting congregation, perhaps not tired out, but
too sure of self, pretending buoyancy where there might
have been transformation. There is the voice that takes the
old script and renders it to evoke a new world we had not
yet witnessed (cf. Isa. 43:19). The fourth and final partner
is *this better world* given as fresh revelation. Something is
revealed, we know not how: a probe behind the closed
parameters of religion too-long settled and politics too-
easily comfortable. It is not only truth disclosed, but it is
life disclosed.[20] Life unclosed, life made open, certitudes
broken so that we can redecide, images moving, imagination assaulting ideology.[21] We find new configurations of
life yet unformed, unthought, but now available. The old
slogans sound unconvincing. I thought I had come for
certitude, but the poetic speech does not give certitude. As
I am addressed by the gospel, I hear anew that possibility
overwhelms necessity in my life. The only available absolute given me is a "fiction" to which I must trust myself—a
gracious "fiction" on which I stake my life, authored by
God who also authors the text and the speech.

The congregation departs. Same old quarrels in the
car on the way home. Same old tensions at dinner. Same
tired beginning on Monday. Now, however, there is disclosed a new word, a new hope, a new verb, a new conversation, a new risk, a new possibility. It is not a new
truth, but rather one long known that had been greatly
reduced. That long-known truth is now greatly enhanced
in riches, texture, availability, demand. My life is mapped
in mystery and I accept that new life; but it is also mapped
in vulnerability and it frightens me. The mystery gives

regal authority and freedom in the face of an IRS audit. The vulnerability permits me to come out from behind my desk, my stethoscope, my uniform, my competence, my credentials, my fears—to meet life a little more boldly. Yet again, as the word is spoken one more time, we move through the wearisome death-ridden days of our life and come back once again to Easter to be stunned into disbelief, and then beyond disbelief, to be stunned to life, now filled with fear and trembling.

The meeting involves this old text, the spent congregation believing but impoverished, the artist of new possibility, the disclosure. The Prince of Darkness tries frantically to keep the world closed so that we can be administered. The Prince has such powerful allies in this age. Against such enormous odds, however, there is the working of this feeble, inscrutable, unshackled moment of sermon. Sometimes the Prince will win the day and there is no new thing uttered or heard. Sometimes, however, the sermon will have its say and the truth looms large— larger than the text or the voice or the folk had any reason to expect. When that happens, the world is set loose toward healing. The sermon for such a time shames the Prince and we become yet again more nearly human. The Author of the text laughs in delight, the way that Author has laughed only at creation and at Easter, but laughs again when the sermon carries the day against the prose of the Dark Prince who wants no new poetry in the region he thinks he governs. Where the poetry is sounded, the Prince knows a little of the territory has been lost to its true Ruler. The newly claimed territory becomes a new home of freedom, justice, peace, and abiding joy. This happens when the poet comes, when the poet speaks, when the preacher comes as poet.

Numbness and Ache

The Strangeness of Healing

The preacher is called to weave an artistic connection between the text in its elusive, liberated truth, and the congregation in its propensity to hear the text in forms of reductionism.[1] That task requires articulation of a great truth in the text that may be unnoticed reality in the congregation—unnoticed, or noticed and rejected, or routinized. Preaching makes it possible for something that has been closed to be powerfully disclosed. My concern here is with the powerful reality of guilt and the more powerful reality of healing. The artistry of the preacher must disclose both the power of guilt and of healing, and then lead the congregation through the delicate transaction whereby healing overcomes and overrides guilt.

In addressing the theme of guilt and healing, the preacher has a threefold task of articulation. First, the preacher is to explicate the reality, power, destructiveness, and hurt that comes with sin and its accompanying guilt. That reality is more powerful and more destructive than we are wont to imagine. Second, the preacher is to construe an alternative. The biblical text trusts and asserts that reconciliation, forgiveness, and restoration are

indeed possible. It is possible to live in blessed communion. It is the promise of the text, and the God of the text,
that there is a way out of alienation to genuine communion: "Before they call I will answer, while they are yet
speaking I will hear" (Isa. 65:24). The alternative offered in
this text and many others is a relation in which all the
breakage is restored and the hurt is healed. The Bible is
rich in its modes of speaking about earth restored to fruition (Ezek. 36:30, Amos 9:13-15) about healed hearts
(Ezek. 36:26) and healed cities (Isa. 54:11, Jer. 31:18-22),
about covenants restored (Jer. 31:31-34) and strangers
come home (Isa. 43:5-7), about all-inclusive banquets
(Luke 14:15-24) and wayward ones given their birthright
(Luke 15:22-24). The Bible poses the alternatives clearly:
the deathly reality of guilt and the news of life undiminished. The preacher's task is to make the second alternative real and winsome—authorized and authorizing—in
the face of ideologies that want to deny, dismiss, and preclude.

    The third task of articulation for the preacher is to
trace and voice the delicate, tortured, dramatic way in
which God moves for and with us from one world to the
other, a move wrought in love and faithfulness, but also
wrought in grief and humiliation. This move is made possible by steadfastness and solidarity we know nowhere
else. The tricky part for all of us is the astonishing mystery
of moving from here to there. The move is beyond our
discernment, but the preacher must find a way to bring it
to speech.[2]

    This threefold task of articulation is so difficult pre-
cisely because these claims are already known in the
church. They are, however, frequently known in such
reductionist ways. The whole drama of guilt and forgiveness—of old death and new life—is present and discerned in two terribly destructive forms. One is the notion
that we live in a world of strict retribution. In order for the
world to be coherent, each person must receive the pay-
offs of his or her acts, and so we are deeply judged and

ultimately fated. The punishment lingers without relief. Or conversely, grace is as reduced as guilt; we imagine that God can easily "by the blood" write off sin, and things are made okay. These two reductions of hard judgment and soft grace haunt contemporary popular faith.

We know, however, that genuine love and real forgiveness do not work in such mechanical fashion. The urgent truth—the truth so hard to voice—is that the drama of guilt and grace does not happen in some automatic or mechanical way. It happens only through the fabric of care and suffering whereby God enters into every cubit of the process. Speech about this mystery of healing requires a language other than the hard legalism or the easy psychologism so much around us. The artful drama of hurt healed requires an artful voice that stands shrewdly against the voices that either make guilt our fate, or that offer healing too soon and too cheaply.

Guilt and Alienation Uncovered, Made Audible

So who is out there? The preacher addresses people with layers and layers of alienation that result from sin and that are experienced as guilt. The gathered congregation includes those who are profoundly burdened with guilt, whose lives are framed by deep wrong, by skewed relations beyond resolve, shareholders in the public drama of brutality and exploitation. There is a heaviness, and pious good humor is not an adequate response. The heaviness is poorly matched by yearning, but there is a yearning nonetheless. It is the resilience of the yearning that causes people to dress up in their heaviness and present themselves for the drama one more time. Sunday morning is, for some, a last, desperate hope that life need not be lived in alienation. We need not dwell on the sin that produces alienation. Suffice with Karl Marx and Sigmund Freud to say that sin characteristically is manifested in distorted relations to sex and money, in lust and in greed, in abuse of neighbor and in the squandering of creation. As the guilt emerges, alienation lingers. And the desperation resulting from the alienation lingers even more powerfully.

The alienation and guilt linger so long, so hopelessly, so powerfully, that one must eventually bury them. We bury them in order to get on with our life as best we can. We may bury them in "can-do theology," bury them in a facade of autonomous indifference, bury them in resignation. Guilt and alienation are givens, however, that will not be denied. Bury alienation and guilt in numbness and after a while one does not notice. So Jeremiah says,

> Everyone is greedy for unjust gain . . .
> They heal lightly saying "Peace, peace,"
> when there is no peace.
> They did not know how to blush.
>
> (Jer. 6:13-15)

The poet understands the reality and power of the temptation to bury. The poet therefore addresses Israel's sin directly and unflinchingly. The inventory offered by the poet Jeremiah begins in greed: "Everyone is greedy for unjust gain." The poem could as easily have begun with lust (as happens in Jer. 5:8; 13:27).[3] The cover-up made by Israel is an unblushing assurance: "Peace, peace." "I am fine, pastor. Everything is OK." We lie long enough and we forget to blush.[4]

Israel has become incongruous with the God who creates, loves, and summons. Communion with God has become impossible. Israel, however, does not notice, and has not noticed for so long that Israel is immobilized and cannot respond, even in shame. Israel buries the incongruity and the loss of wholeness and settles for pretense: "Peace, peace." "America is back." "The market has bottomed out." "It doesn't get any better than this." Israel did not notice. The poet notices though, and cannot remain silent.

The preacher must address that which is buried, because even when hidden, the alienation remains powerful and destructive. Guilt lingers unnoticed. It reduces

us to automatons: weary, cynical, resigned. Resignation
causes failed communication. Not only do we not talk to
Fidel Castro, having ended diplomatic relations, but we
also do not talk to wife or husband or children either. We
have been over the same ground of buried guilt so many
times and accepted it in our lives so long we have labeled
it "normalcy." We come on Sunday morning with a desperate yearning to move past that lingering immobiliza-
tion. Guilt, unaddressed, will finally kill. We come to
church even in our convinced secularity. We know that
alienation must be addressed, and we yearn to have it
addressed. We still faintly recall that God is indeed God.
The surface fact that I may believe only in a diminished
God does not keep the burden of alienation and the yearning for forgiveness from operating powerfully in my life.
Even in our failure to blush, we yearn for the incongruity
to be overcome.

Believers whose faith is greatly diminished may
utter a truth greatly reduced: "Smile, God loves you."
Does God love because God is engaged in some cover-up
with us and does not know about the alienation? Because
if God knew, God would not meet me with a smile, but
with a deep, deep cry for life run amiss. The alienation is
heavy, serious, and burdensome for us, because it is
heavy, serious, and burdensome for the alienated father
God, for the mother God who grieves for us while we are
too numb to grieve.

The preacher can open up this greatly reduced
truth of guilt. The preacher over time articulates a new
taxonomy of guilt and grace. Over time, what happens on
Sunday morning is an artistic rendering of a new truth-
filled world in which many people may come to live and
begin to function again with the freedom that belongs
peculiarly to God's children. "Finally comes the poet" to
sing the songs of God, and then God's children join the
song of life. But it will not happen, until finally comes the
poet, the one who speaks honestly about the incongruity,
who speaks buoyantly about the alternative.

A Move Beginning in Prophetic Disclosure

In what follows, I will sketch a taxonomy of an Old Testament understanding of guilt and healing. That is, the several literatures of the Old Testament present various elements of that understanding. No one text presents the entire scope of the issue or its resolution. I will suggest a sequence of categories that shows how these elements from the various literatures are dynamically interrelated in a processive whole. It is that processive whole that the preacher brings to poetic articulation and that the congregation enacts in its liturgy.

1. The drama of guilt and forgiveness, when engaged in its undiminished power, does not begin with how we feel. *It begins in candor at the throne of God.* It begins with what God notices and how God responds. What God notices, and we notice in God's presence, is that life so often is lived sideways, in violation of Torah, in violation of every real possibility for community and communion. God notices and then Israel notices. I will consider Jeremiah 5 as a poetic scenario through which the notice of God is voiced in Israel. The poet has God say:

> Your iniquities have turned these away,
>   and your sins have kept good from you.
> For wicked men are found among my people;
>   they lurk like fowlers lying in wait.
> They set a trap;
>   they catch men.
> Like a basket full of birds,
>   their houses are full of treachery;
> therefore they have become great and rich,
>   they have grown fat and sleek.
> They know no bounds in deeds of wickedness;
>   they judge not with justice
> the cause of the fatherless, to make it prosper,
>   and they do not defend the rights of the needy.
>   (Jer. 5:25-28)

To be sure, this is a tough, demanding text. Perhaps it is too tough to bear, or even to utter. The wonder is that it is a text that has been preserved in our community. It is a text to which the church has sworn allegiance. Therefore, in order to confront the truth greatly reduced, the preacher does not need to rail and scold, but only to let the text be present among us, addressing our true situation. Guilt is not simply a psychological problem, but it concerns the realities of abuse. God notices the abuse; so God says, "Shall I not punish them for these things?" (v. 29). In the role of preacher we are not to be clinical therapists, but poets to render the God who knows and notices, who speaks and responds.[5] If one wants to get at social ethics and social change, one must begin with the theological reality and the abuse of God. The poets of Israel are clear that sin, which produces deathly guilt, concerns the reality of God and our refusal to come to terms with God's goodness.[6]

In the candid speech of the poet, God knows about our depths of alienation. Our life is lived in the presence of the God "from whom no secret can be hid." In the presence of that God, my numb denial and my jaded resignation are inappropriate. They are inappropriate in the presence of this God who already knows.

2. After God notices the truth about us (voiced by the poet), God responds to that truth. The poem of Jeremiah 5 continues with a presentation of God's response. The taxonomy of guilt and healing includes two dimensions of God's response to the reality of sin and guilt. *First there is God's wrath, indignation, and anger.* The prophets speak powerfully, redundantly, and without apology about God's anger. Heaven is genuinely offended by our distorted ways of living. We have nonetheless come to present ourselves to the throne, because we know we belong there and finally must go there.

God's anger is known among us, but again in ways harshly reduced. As noted, God's anger is conventionally reduced to mechanistic retributive principles of punishment, as though certain acts automatically produce reactions of punishment. What is missing in such a picture of

reductionism is that this is our God, our progenitor, our
hoper who is affronted.[7] The very God who gives us
unspeakable gifts is the affronted party. Because of such
gifts abused, prophetic rage bespeaks the hurt that our
waywardness on earth evokes in heaven. Judgment that is
not understood as a form of unendurable hurt misses the
point of the biblical drama.

The truth greatly reduced is that we are under judgment. The truth artistically disclosed is that the throne
room of heaven is filled with alarm that the rule of life is
mocked in the province where we live. The news of that
earthly mockery has now reached the throne room. This
government over which Yahweh presides will not be
mocked, because such mocking will bring death. And
heaven is aimed toward life.

The mockery of God accomplished through distorted actions evokes harshness from God's throne, which
is brought to speech by the daring poets of Israel. In the
poetry of Jeremiah, God does not meet us in love, but is
utterly aghast. Being God is serious business. God is not
indifferent to the attitude and actions of God's subjects.
Thus after a catalogue of the affronts, during which we
can only plead *nolo contendere,* this God says: "How can I
pardon you?" (Jer. 5:7) That is, I would, but I cannot:
"Shall I not punish you, Shall I not avenge myself on a
nation such as this?" (Jer. 5:9, 29)

This speech of God is not a harangue. It is the
poet's bold glimpse into the heart of God. The poet
enables us to see that God notices how we live and is
deeply troubled. If God has noticed so clearly that we act
in destructive ways, then I also am free to notice—to stop
the pretense. If God had not noticed, then I might
usefully continue to pretend. But God has noticed. If
heaven is brought to a momentary halt by my affront,
then I also can acknowledge that little pieces of my life are
immobilized. Eventually more and more of life has
become frozen and closed in pretense. My life is diminished because I have not noticed or cared or responded. I

cannot afford to notice because it hurts too much, it unsettles, and it frightens. Yet when God notices, I remember to blush as I have not done, because now I am in the presence of one who is embarrassed for me and with me. Perhaps the first sign that the numbness may subside is given at the throne when I blush deeply again, for the first time in a long time. I blush in the presence of the God who is so troubled over me. I learn, as I had forgotten, that my life has moral significance at the throne of God.[8] I am permitted to blush as I have not for a long time. The blushing is evoked by the seriousness with which God regards me.

3. Along with anger, God makes a second response to our guilt. *Anger at the throne is compounded by God's utter anguish at having hoped and been betrayed, at having yearned and failed.* The indignant judge is yet the pitiful mother and the grieving father. Finally our guilt causes not indignation but deep hurt at the throne.

The father in the throne room speaks in this way:

I thought how I would set you among my sons
and give you a pleasant land,
a heritage most beauteous of all the nations.
I thought you would call me, "My Father,"
and would not turn from following after me.
(Jer. 3:19)

When you were a little child, I dreamed of your growing up and how we would have life together. I have worked all my life so that yours would be good. But you have been faithless, even like a fickle wife in a bad marriage (v. 20). The father God grieves in wistfulness.

From the throne, this same God speaks as a mother:

Is Ephraim my dear son?
    Is he my darling child?
For as often as I speak against him,
    I do remember him still.
Therefore my heart yearns for him.
    I will surely have mercy on him, says the Lord.
(Jer. 31:20)[9]

The father spoke in yearning, but finally quit in dismay at the betrayal. After the voice of the father has become silent, then comes the voice of the mother who finds that she cannot turn loose of her beloved child.

The same reality may be voiced in a very different metaphor. When this God finally receives the word of terminal illness, that the partner will die, God is moved like any caring covenant partner:

> O that my head were waters,
>   and my eyes a fountain of tears,
> that I might weep day and night
>   for the slain of the daughter of my people!
> (Jer. 9:1)

This response of God, dear friends, is going on now while we do not notice. The judge remembers to be a parent: a father in wistfulness, a mother in yearning, a God of grief flowing with tears beside the deathbed. The angry God remembers to be a God who cares about the beloved partner. God has noticed. God has noticed the mocking and the dying, the denial and the irrepressible pain.

To be sure, the oracle Jeremiah places in God's mouth is only a poem. Yet "finally comes the poet." Jeremiah's rendering (and ours after this poet) offers an artistic shaping of reality that asks no ontological questions, but wants the listener to be present to the poem. God's caring grief assures that the ultimate transactions about guilt and fickleness are not reduced to cynical resignations that immobilize or to alienations that are endless. The poem is not simply convenient rhetoric. It moves powerfully underneath our conventional categories to disclose what has been firmly closed. What is closed is any relation Israel had with Yahweh. It is closed in deathliness. It is now, on the lips of the poet, Yahweh's anguished love that breaks that closure, that uncloses, that discloses, that opens hurt to new possibility.

A Move Ending in Priestly Resolve

Thus far we have focused on the dark realities of guilt, anger, and hurt. In the characteristic dramatic sequence of Israel's life with God, now there may be a move to newness. The drama of guilt and grace takes a new turn.

1. In this drama of truth undiminished, the response of God given in these poems of Jeremiah invites this question: what will you do (cf. Acts 2:37)? It is a hopeful question. To be sure, a new move is required. The important assertion, however, is that *a new move can be made from our side*. The tears of the judge permit a new choice on this side, a choice that has not been made by us for a very long time, a choice of obedience, devotion, and self-giving. The truth known by the poet is that the tears of the judge permit a new move. If the judge had spoken only in harshness, the people of God would be fated. But the tears of the judge have cracked the fate the stern judge might impose. It may seem strange, but I propose that the reality of guilt moves us from prophet to priest, finally from the poetry of Jeremiah to the cultic apparatus of the Book of Leviticus. The neglected Book of Leviticus is a long study on the good news that God has indeed provided ways through the paralysis of guilt.[10] I consider now a text that imagines beyond God's anger and anguish to receive the offer of forgiveness through acts of worship (Lev. 6:1-7).

Leviticus 6:1-7 is a remarkable text to find in the priestly routinations of Leviticus. Indeed, it is a remarkable text to find anywhere. I propose it as a model for dealing with the powerful reality of guilt and the more powerful reality of healing. It begins, like all good healing, with a diagnosis:

> If any one sins and commits a breach of faith against the Lord by deceiving his neighbor in a matter of deposit or security, or through robbery, or if he has oppressed his neighbor or has found what was lost and lied about it, swearing falsely . . . .

The text gets down to cases. The text knows that most of our distorted life concerns pushing and shoving the neighbor about goods which one has and another wants. The Bible is realistic. Guilt is not disposed of quickly as though it were a problem without persistent visible consequence. The text shrewdly recognizes that breach of faith against Yahweh concerns securities and deposits, stocks and bonds, transactions of worth, value, property, and power. Violations of God's covenant are acted out in the routine realities of human community. This linkage of violation of God and violation of neighbor is found not only in Amos but also in Leviticus, not only in the rage of prophets but also in the ache of priests.

The connection between Yahweh and economics is a bold and persistent one in the Bible, because the Bible knows that economics is one of the two spheres where we live our life. The violation is rendered artistically in this text, not focused on an economic issue, but on pain and hurt and exploitation. The pain, hurt, and violation in this text concern taking what belongs to another, e.g., power relations in the family, robbing the value of another life by sexism, racism, or ageism. Or turn the metaphor to Central America and notice how well we live from food taken from the table of a peasant. It is dawning on us slowly that in both El Salvador and Nicaragua we are concerned with long-term U.S. robbery that we have come to think of as business as usual, as we enjoy the fruit of the United Fruit Company.[11] How strange to have a "ritual text," so conventionally ignored by us, become so immediately available for the scary places in our life that have to do with problems of guilt and alienation.

After the diagnosis of neighbor violation, the text recognizes that guilt requires action on our part in response to God's anger and God's anguish. One must do something about the guilt and its destructive power. First, the priests suggest, one must make intentional, concrete reparations. The priests prescribe the response:

> He shall restore what he has taken by robbery or
> what he got by oppression, or the deposit which was
> committed to him, or the lost thing which he found,
> or anything about which he has sworn falsely; he
> shall restore it in full. And shall give it to him to
> whom it belongs, on the day of his guilt offering.
>
> (Lev. 6:4-5)

Justice is the discernment of what belongs to whom, and returning it to them.[12] We all have goods that belong to others. Guilt requires concrete, explicit, intentional action of reparations. The theme is inflammatory. Many remember the trembling that James Foreman caused. Old debts must be settled, old debts that have been wrought either personally or systematically. That is why we pray to have debts forgiven and why we forgive debtors.[13] The possibility of forgiveness is good news because it affirms that we are not helpless with our guilt. We can act to deal with it. We can make amends (cf. Jer. 7:3). Such amends, however, require moving beyond numb resignation to take responsibility for the burden.

Restitution costs: "He shall restore it in full, and shall add a fifth to it." Restitution costs twenty percent according to Leviticus. Guilt requires not simply equity and an even balance, but gift beyond affront. It requires surplus compensation. Such a rule is both economically shrewd and psychologically sound. Israel is required to move beyond grudging restoration, until it is "pressed down and running over."

This Leviticus text speaks specifically of distorted economic relations. In terms of reparations, however, we may extend the teaching of the text to personal and interpersonal relations as well. The metaphor of reparations applies wherever there has been violation of another member of the community. Every act of violation, this text asserts, requires concrete, intentional reparation, in interpersonal as well as in public issues. Preaching voices the requirement of reparation necessary for reconciliation and

the recovery of life. The text of Leviticus 6 makes clear that
human guilt is not some mystifying power beyond the
reach of human responsibility. The requirement of reparation, made explicit in the text, invites us beyond our conventional resignation in the face of guilt. Not only must
something be done. Something may be done to move
toward reconciliation. We are not left helpless in the face
of guilt, massive though it may be. We can act! This text
brings to speech the requirement necessary to recover life.

    2. According to our Leviticus text, there are two
things to be done about guilt. The first is reparation, done
by the offender. This is the move from the human side.
The second is more difficult, because we cannot do it ourselves. It must be done for us. *There is a weighty residue of
ache that one cannot dispel by one's own actions.*[14] The affront
and its resolution are more troublesome and more profound than we ourselves can settle. What remains unre-
solved is underneath guilt; it is more like taintedness,
uncleanness. The priests noticed that even after adequate
reparations are done, one is not yet finished. The problem
of alienation lingers. The priests did not shrink from the
recognition that this unfinished business requires them to
act as priests. There is an authority they will have to exercise, costly as it is. Priests, even those who think of themselves primarily as preachers, are entrusted with this
"residue of ache" that is dealt with only through mystery
that reaches from the other side, out where we cannot act
reasonably or effectively. Finally, guilt requires God's
action. That action of God, in order to be reliably available,
must be given by the regularized channels of priestly
action. The work of priests is to make available the God
who is required for reconciliation.

    The problem for the text, and for the ongoing com-
munity of worship and interpretation, is how to speak of
God's action that is given as priestly action. God's action
wrought by the priests is an action of God's pure gift, but
it is a gift done through the offering given by the worshiper. God's action wrought by the priests is a visible,

concrete act, but it is an act with surplus meanings that move well beyond what is visible and concrete. The language for God's act wrought through the priests is the language of sacrament, an invisible act wrought through a visible sign, a means of grace wrought through the concreteness of human offering. The text of Leviticus has finished with human reparation and now speaks of God's sacramental activity.

Because of the very character of sacrament, textual speech about sacrament cannot be direct, frontal speech. Sacrament requires speech that concerns elusive, symbolic gestures in which the participants discern more than is visible to an outsider. The act of sacrament requires the speech of poetry to keep hidden what must not be profaned by description. In this text, the self-giving of God is kept hidden in talk about animals and sacrifices. The parties to this transaction, however, priests and worshipers, are clear that this is not merely an act of animal sacrifice. The animal is the means for sacrament. The animal given is the sign of the self-giving of God, whose self-giving is required for a new beginning.

The Leviticus text speaks of the sign and gift in this way:

> He shall bring to the priest his guilt offering to the Lord, a ram without blemish out of the flock, valued by you at the price for a guilt offering. And the priest shall make atonement for him before the Lord, and he shall be forgiven for any of the things which one may do and thereby become guilty.
>
> (Lev. 6:6-7)

This remarkable text may sound strangely archaic to us. In matters of guilt, however, we are archaic creatures who have not "outgrown" the need for action outside ourselves. Indeed, we are more archaic than our modernity and the "freedom myths" of the Enlightenment would have us believe. What the priests in ancient Israel know is that the ache that is left from guilt, even after reparations, cannot be removed by good works, by willpower, by positive thinking, or by romantic psychology. The ache can be removed only by entry into the sphere of the holy, which is not easy or obvious. We cannot give enough to resolve the guilt. Such guilt requires the self-giving of God.

I know of no more probing, poignant articulation of the deep yearning for forgiveness, both in its problematic and possibility, than the discerning narrative of Iris Murdoch, *The Red and the Green*. Murdoch portrays Barney as a mixed-up, dysfunctional Irishman who has sought refuge in too many unworkable alliances.[15] Barney, so the story goes, has lived in too many fickle and duplicitous relationships. Nothing seems to work for him, and he finds each new relation more destructive than the last. Finally, utterly bereft of possibility and disheveled, he staggers into a church on Maundy Thursday. There he pauses before the mystery of altar and sacrament. He reflects in his anguish about the promises of the church and the reality of his own life. He is under no illusions. He wants so much to receive the forgiveness that is offered. He wonders how it could be. He yearns and he resists. The burden of his situation causes him to penetrate the mystery of self-giving of which he can barely conceive:

> How can guilt be taken away, how can it not drag the guilty one down and down? Did redemption exist, *could* it exist, was it not a strictly senseless idea? Could another save me by his suffering? If someone who is good suffers because I am evil and I see and contemplate that suffering, might that not alter me and purify me almost automatically? But such contemplation is possible precisely because I am evil. Human beings cannot look at affliction with uncorrupted eyes . . . .
>
> The chapel was dark and silent and empty . . . Barney looked at the light. The last thing he remembered before sleeping was that piercing approach, *Vinea mea electa*. . . . It seemed to him that it was the most annihilating reproach in the whole world. Yet why was it so? Because it was also, in a way which

one could not possibly mistake, the voice of love. Could reproach and love become so nearly identical? Yes, for this is the nature of the magnet by which what is good draws what is partly evil, by which perhaps mysteriously it may even draw what is wholly evil. . . .

Barney returned to his knees . . . .It must be very late now, perhaps it was already the morning of Good Friday. He stared at the sanctuary light and felt the certain, almost bodily, presence of perfect Goodness. And with this he felt, as he had not felt it before, an absolute certainty of his own existence. He existed and God, opposite to him, existed too. And if he was not, by that juxtaposition, simply dissolved into things, it could only be because God was love . . . .

He could make everything simple and innocent once again, and in that instant he knew too that if he lifted so much as a finger to attempt that simplicity and that innocence he would receive, from the other region which had seemed so far away outside him, the inrush of an entirely new strength. He had thought himself so lost, so astronomically far removed that there was no nearer or further any more and no sense in the idea of a way. But all the time he had been held so close that he could not escape even if he would.

Barney anguishes over his guilt and his doubt that he can be forgiven. So do we all anguish. So do the people who gather on Sunday morning. As Jeremiah knows about God's anguish, so the priests in Leviticus understand that the resolve of guilt is complex, painful, and demanding. The priests know, concerning the possibility of healing, that:

1. We cannot alone work our own healing. It requires a priest, someone who is authorized in the community, who is recognized as having the capacity to bear and enact holiness among us, holiness that outruns our technical control and understanding.

2. Healing requires the submission of something of value. Entering the place of forgiveness where the priest waits is dangerous, because awe dwells there beyond our

calculation. The place of forgiveness is so ominous that one cannot go there empty-handed. One must give of one's best, as a decisive gesture of submission and relinquishment.

3. Healing is the enactment of atonement (*kpr*), so that the poison of the affront is forever contained and removed as a threat. The poison of guilt is at least as dangerous as nuclear waste. It must be put away where it cannot destroy or contaminate.

4. The act of putting the poison away is an act done not by ourselves but on our behalf by the priest who bears holiness. This act done for us leads to forgiveness, reconciliation, and the capacity to start again with a new life and a restored relation.

The priests in the Leviticus text know that finally guilt requires a sacrifice "from the other side," from the very person of God who alone has enough self to give to answer the guilt. Such sacrifice, however, cannot be enacted directly, because God is not so directly available. The sacrifice therefore is enacted "at a distance." The distance is maintained by the use of the animal; the participants know, however, that it is the very presence of God that overrides the distance, that contacts directly and decisively the poisonous power of guilt. Israel has no other speech available for the miracle of restoration. The language of sacrifice is ultimately inadequate for the miracle of God's self-gift, because the disjunction between sacrificed animal and God's self-gift is great and deep. By its careful poetic nurture, however, Israel found this language adequate to say what needed to be said, and to do what needed to be done. What Israel says and does in this priestly scenario points to what God is saying and doing in God's act of self-giving.

The vehicle for Israel's speech and action is "blood," the life-blood, the very embodiment of self. It takes life-blood to answer for our guilt. The priestly routines administered that act of blood-gift. We, however, should not miss the theological affirmation in the act. The gift is the gift of holy blood. In the end, the act signifies the self-gift of God. It is only this gift of life that answers for our guilt. Nothing else could do what needs to be done.

That enormous insight of the gospel of God's self-gift has been greatly reduced in two characteristic ways. On the one hand, priestly sacrifice is treated simply as animal sacrifice, and it is forgotten that the priests refer to nothing less than the life of God given in this act. On the other hand, the act is reduced to a slogan, "saved by the blood." The slogan fails to remember that it is life poured out in costly ways. The slogan makes God's rescue of the guilty seem routine and undemanding. Against such reductions, the Levitical priests act out the self-giving of God, done in deep hurt, and out of great yearning and caring and loving.

Murdoch's Barney, along with the entire Christian tradition, refers to this priestly act of self-giving as "Good Friday." The name of the day and of the event of self-gift is a polemical name. It dares to call good what the world would surely call bad. To give self for another is a good thing, a good gift on a good day, because it is the only way we can live in the midst of our morass of broken relations. It is the goodness of that day that overrides our numbness and God's rage, that transcends our reparations and waits for the one thing we cannot do for ourselves. It is no wonder that Murdoch and the priests of Leviticus must resort to poetic language and action. How else speak about the reality beyond us that gives us life again? That reality is none other than the aching love of God, which moves against our ache for the sake of newness.

One of the tasks of the preacher is to speak the community through this taxonomy of guilt and healing. It is folly to imagine that modern people do not struggle with the reality of guilt and the yearning for healing. The pathos-filled verbal aches of Jeremiah and the regularized resolutions of the Levitical priests enable the preacher to bring this reality of our lives to poetic speech. The preacher is entrusted with these truths that dare not be reduced:

- The reality of God: *God notices* and is attentive to the deep human quandary (Jer. 6:13-15; 5:25-28);
- The God who notices and takes guilt seriously, *responds in anger and indignation* (Jer. 5:7, 9, 29);
- God notices and *responds in pathos and grief,* and is beset by profound disappointment (Jer. 3:19; 9:1; 31:20);
- *Reparations are specified* which require intentional action toward neighbor (Lev. 6:4-5);
- The residue of ache is dealt with by *sacramental action* that mediates to us God's own life given toward us (Lev. 6:6-7).[16]

The anguish of our preaching is that these truths are frequently reduced in ways that rob the gospel of its power and urgency. We have the perspective of romantic psychology that concludes that I am not guilty but only "feel" guilty. And because the problem is not taken seriously, no serious response can be entertained. Such a conclusion, of course, only buries the alienation at deeper levels. Or we may approach guilt and healing through ethical self-confidence, that is, I can rectify what is wrong by doing better and keeping my life moral. This conclusion is big on reparations, but is unaware of the power of the ache that endures after all the reparations are made. Such a posture requires a deep denial of the alienation. Or we may attempt to pay up at church and so imagine some benefit without having to face the reality. Or in a secular version, to pay up in the market or in the academy in ways of responsibility and competence. Such a conclusion resists the notion of self-giving from another on my behalf.

None of these reductions is adequate, however, even though they have become respectable conventions among us. They are not adequate because they constitute a truth greatly reduced. The truth of guilt and healing as we know it in the context of the gospel includes: the reality of God in anger and anguish, never only one, but always both; the requirement of reparations; and the resolve of the residue of ache that we ourselves cannot resolve.

This move from guilt to healing as found in the taxonomy from Jeremiah and Leviticus affirms the reality of God's rage, God's hurt, God's ache, and God's self-giving love. The panoply of God's rage, hurt, ache, and love is an awesome dramatic reality in the life of faith. It overrides all other presumed reality. Our task in preaching is to find ways for the enactment of this awesome drama of self-gift. The truth of God's ways with the guilty is no common, routine reality. Our speech about it can be no common, routine speech, but must be utterly uncommon. That is why the claim for God requires poetic speech, speech that is costly and demanding. Such speech costs us. The reality costs those who listen and the God about whom we speak.

On Neighbor-Love and God's Self-Giving

This taxonomy of guilt and healing is a central theme for the preacher. The Old Testament provides crucial materials for speech about this life-and-death drama of self-giving. The same taxonomy is present in the New Testament. Here I will consider two texts in juxtaposition that also speak of reparation and residue. The first of these texts concerns the requirement of reparations, a requirement not unlike that in Leviticus 6. The second text speaks of God's resolve of the residue of guilt and ache that even the reparations cannot touch.

Matt. 5:23-26. In the Sermon on the Mount, Jesus teaches about the new righteousness, about the capacity to order life in new ways.[17] It is the hope and promise of the gospel that the community of Jesus could practice a more faithful, life-giving righteousness. In the catalogue for this mandate, Jesus asserts that anger with a brother or sister makes one subject to judgment:

> So if you are offering your gift at the altar, and then remember that your brother has something against

you, leave your gift before the altar and go, first be
reconciled to your brother and then come and offer
your gift.

The new righteousness offered in the gospel occurs in a
world where people like us are angry enough to kill. People who are angry enough to kill do come to church, do
approach God, do bring an offering. Jesus asserts that the
making of reparations precedes offerings to God. Neighbor is the prerequisite for communion with God. Well-
being among earthlings is a precondition for access to
heaven. So go to your brother, your sister, the ones you
have wronged. That reconciliation is a human act, done
before approaching the throne. God's judgment, anger,
and indignation require a full, risky presentation of self to
the sister or the brother. The work of reconciliation is
human work to be done by those who are guilty. That is
the same reparation the priests of Leviticus knew about.

Then, only then, the offering must and may be
brought to God. The required offering, however, is not
simply an act of reparations. The offering is a point of
access where the mystery of God's work moves over us in
ways that we do not understand. The offering is an
enactment of whose we are, to whom we belong, who we
trust. Healing entails getting clear on who we are by
reference to the God who becomes the decisive actor in
the healing process.

Jesus' teaching acknowledges the two acts that are
crucial for our humanness. The two acts belong together.
They cannot be separated from each other. They have,
moreover, a necessary sequence. First there is reparations.
The neighbor must be dealt with. Then there is an offer of
self to God, and in that offer, we enter into new communion. These two acts together are essential in moving past
alienation to new life with God, in God's world. The
promise of such an act is to be free for life in the world.

Heb. 10:19-23. The rich poetic language of the letter
to the Hebrews begins at a different point. The world in its

need has been visited by God. God is moved from alienation to pathos, knowing that we cannot offer enough reparations to right the wrong. Therefore God must intercede. It is God's self-giving love, God's yearning, God's care that deals with the residue of human ache. This Hebrews text does not talk about human action and reparations. Its lyrical wording invites us to be amazed and grateful for the initiative God has taken toward us.

The question left from Leviticus 6 is: Where shall I get a ram with no blemish, because everything I have is caught in the blemish? Mine is a blemished life and nothing is exempt. Yet we have long known, as Abraham told his son, that "God would provide" an adequate ram to serve reconciliation (Gen. 22:8).

That offer of the ram is the preaching point in Heb. 19:19-23:

> Therefore brethren, since we have confidence to enter the sanctuary by the blood of Jesus, by the new and living way which he opened for us through the curtain, that is, through his flesh, and since we have a great high priest over the house of God, let us draw near with a true heart in full assurance of faith, with our hearts sprinkled clean from an evil conscience and our bodies washed with pure water. Let us hold fast the confession of our hope without wavering, for he who promised is faithful.

The text urges the faithful who may be tempted to other offers of well-being. Do not sell out. Hold fast to the hope. The ground for holding fast is not simply determination and will-power, nor is the basis for courage in reparations. The ground for hope is that the residue of ache about our "evil conscience" to which we have no remedial access has been handled in another way (v. 22).[18] The blood of Jesus has opened the "new and living way" (v. 20). His own flesh (self) lets us come near (vv. 20-22). This priest whom we have anticipated in Leviticus 6 now does what we cannot do for ourselves. The priest who offers the sacrifice in Leviticus has become, in

Hebrews 10, the one who gives self in our behalf. The priest's self-giving is a gesture of God's self-giving in our behalf.

It sounds strange for us in mainline Protestantism to be saying such things. Nonetheless the requirement of reparation and the self-giving by God constitute the central insight of the gospel. Real guilt requires real repentance. Finally, however, guilt requires a flood of "self-gift" from one outside ourselves. This gift overwhelms us, because the one who gives self stands in solidarity with us at great cost. *Evangelical faith is a study of how God is more for us than we are for ourselves* (cf. Rom. 8:31-39). It is the very life of God that deals with the lingering poison of our "evil conscience," poison that causes death to us and to those around us. God's way with us emerges out of God's deep love that cannot stand by while we die of the poison. In the priestly version of God's care, it is God's blood, God's self, God's own life, God's love that is passionately, generously, recklessly thrown across the poison of guilt.

Evangelical preaching is invited to break out of the conservatism that makes God function mechanically, for such a scholastic God has no power to save. Preaching is invited to break out of the liberalism that believes we finally can manage on our own, for managing never gives life. Preaching has to do with a life poured out for us to deal with the residue of guilt left untouched by reparations.

We who are children of these odd texts meet together on Sunday morning to acknowledge and enact these realities that give life. The juxtaposition of *reparations and residue* is a difficult and interesting question. In the Sermon on the Mount (Matt. 5:23-26), reparations are put before sacrifice. Things must be right first with the neighbor. But in Hebrews 10:19-23, the residue of death is resolved in the only way it can be—by God who generously overrides the guilt at the great risk and cost of God's very own life.

The Making of All Well

These two emphases of reparation and residue run throughout Scripture. The experience of these two runs throughout our life. We are creatures engaged in guilt management, because we do not fully know how the poison may be resolved. It seldom dawns on us that the chance for another life comes only by the other One who, out of love, is placed fully in jeopardy for us.

Such an inscrutable resolution of guilt must be articulated poetically, because the reality of God's self-giving outruns all our capacities to speak about it. We have no language to say fully what we know about God's love, which in self-giving transforms. Unless we speak poetically, we invite terrible reductions. Unless we speak poetically, God's self-giving transformation will be heard as a form of cheap grace that costs God nothing because God simply overrides. Our poetry, however, helps us articulate how costly our new life is for God. Or conversely, without poetry God's transformation of our guilt will be heard as a form of works righteousness, as though some price had to match the affront, whether the "works" are those of God or of us. The truth of our reclamation, however, is not cheap grace that costs God nothing; nor is it simple satisfaction that matches and pays off. It is rather a total giving, out of extravagance, that runs beyond payment, but at deep cost. The preacher, like the text, speaks metaphorically, because it is the only way to break the deadly misunderstandings of our culture, either deadly romanticism that imagines grace is easy, or deadly retribution that allows no free gift.[19]

This taxonomy of guilt and healing, so central to our faith, is difficult and problematic, because it runs against the assumptions of our common cultural self-understanding. It challenges our usual assumptions in at least three ways:

1. Every aspect of what is urged here as a biblical way of understanding and transforming guilt runs against the ideology of our culture. We have made a series of theological affirmations that the world does not easily embrace. We have affirmed:

- that there is real guilt,
- that God is serious in anger and anguish,
- that reparations are required,
- that the residue is resolved.

These points need to be made clearly, carefully, precisely, and well, because these claims violate our presumed world of modernity.

2. This way of reading our human situation connects things that do not seem to be connected. Thus we have linked together the reality of God's anger with the requirement of reparations. We have linked together the reality of God's pathos with God's "self-gift" against the poison. In both moves—from anger to reparations, from pathos to residue—connections are made between the very character of God and the practice of our life, between the substance of heaven and the reality of earth. The people who listen are waiting for the claim of that connection and how it will be nuanced. It will not do to render the mystery of rehabilitation simply as strict retribution. It also, however, will not do to articulate the inscrutable transformation as easy grace. It must therefore be spoken artfully. This taxonomy of guilt and healing demands careful speech because it affirms that our guilt requires our best courage on earth and it evokes the best caring from heaven.

3. Such artful speech serves to break the ideologies that rob us of power for living. Unless this news is artistically presented, the ideology of liberals will only hear social responsibility and reparations. Unless there is artistry in articulation, the ideology of conservatives will only hear "blood atonement." The priests in Leviticus, however, are wiser than our ideologies. I propose, then,

that good preaching must address the quarrelsome con-
tradiction among us concerning worship and ethics,
priest and prophet, worldliness and sacrament, and
affirm that such dichotomy leaves us more burdened than
we need be.

The preaching of the church may seize the old, deep
memories of frontier hymnody: "Leaning on the Everlast-
ing Arm," "Amazing Grace," and "I Need Thee Every
Hour." These hymns are meditations on the self-giving
blood (self) of God, which makes the world free and ends
the poison. At the same time, however, the preaching of
the church may embrace the great missional claims of
another hymnody: "Where Cross the Crowded Ways of
Life," "In Christ There Is No East or West," "They'll Know
We Are Christians by Our Love," and "We Shall Overcome." When held together, the affirmation of the former
and the hope of the latter make new life possible.[20] Let
preaching be as conservative as it can possibly be about the
self-giving of God who stops the poison. Let the preacher
be as dangerous as she possibly can be about reparations
in the family, in Central America, in all the enslavements
and exploitations we practice. The preacher must be con-
serving of the grace of God and open to the pain and injustice of the world. Neither may be neglected. Both must be
enacted. Only a poet can speak both dimensions of our
dangerous way with God at the throne.

The preaching conversation is the only meeting in
town where these realities will be enacted. The outcome of
such poetic, urgent proclamation might be a church on its
way in glad obedience. Let us consider how to "stir up one
another to love and good works . . . encouraging one
another" (Heb. 10:24-25).

The preacher gives expression to the weight of sin
and to the rage of God. The preacher, however, moves on
to the costly offering of humankind by way of reparation
and to the ache of God which issues in self-giving. The
preacher finally moves on at the end of this dramatic process to give voice to the shape of the new life when we are

"ransomed, healed, restored, forgiven." At the end of this drama, which we relive again and again, we move back from Leviticus to Jeremiah. The tradition of Jeremiah offers a glimpse of the new life that is wrought through God's self-giving.

> Behold, I will restore the fortunes of the tents
>   of Jacob,
>   and have compassion on his dwellings;
> the city shall be rebuilt upon its mound,
>   and the palace shall stand where it used to be.
> Out of them shall come songs of thanksgiving,
>   and the voices of those who make merry;
> I will multiply them, and they shall not be few;
>   I will make them honored, and they shall not be
> small . . . .
> And you shall be my people,
>   and I will be your God.
>
> (Jer. 30:18-22)

> They shall come and sing aloud on the height of Zion,
>   and they shall be radiant over the goodness
>   of the Lord.
> over the grain, the wine, and the oil,
>   and over the young of the flock and the herd;
> their life shall be like a watered garden,
>   and they shall languish no more.
> Then shall the maidens rejoice in the dance,
>   and the young men and the old shall be merry.
> I will turn their mourning into joy,
>   I will comfort them, and give them gladness
>   for sorrow.
>
> (Jer. 31:12-13)

They shall all know me, from the least of them to the greatest, says the Lord; for I will forgive their iniquity, and I will remember their sin no more.

> (Jer. 31:34)

Then shall be heard again the voice of mirth and the voice of gladness, the voice of the bridegroom and the voice of the bride, the voices of those who sing, as they bring shank offerings to the house of the Lord.

> (Jer. 33:10-11)

All will be well with God.[21]

The main claims of these texts, however, do not concern our relationship with God, decisive as that is. Rather, the texts express two anticipations about human life restored. On the one hand, there is anticipation of the restoration of public life, safe cities, caring communities, and secure streets. On the other hand, there is anticipation of the restoration of personal and interpersonal life, happy families, domestic well-being and joy, shared food and delighted relationships. Both public and interpersonal life depend on the self-giving action of God who makes newness possible. This alternative life comes from the self-giving act of atonement wrought only by God.

When the text comes to speak about this alternative life wrought by God, the text must use poetry. There is no other way to speak. We know about that future—we know surely—but we do not know concretely enough to issue memos and blueprints. We know only enough to sing songs and speak poems. That, however, is enough. We stake our lives on such poems.

The preacher renders a world not known in advance. It requires no great cleverness to speak such a world, but it requires closeness to those texts that know secrets that mediate life. These texts voice life that is given nowhere else. The preaching moment is a moment for the gift of God's life in the midst of our tired alienation. For this the church and indeed the world waits. They wait, until, finally the poet comes, until finally the poet comes.

2

Alienation and Rage

The Odd Invitation
to Doxological Communion

To live in blessed communion" is a serious and central promise of the gospel; one day blessed communion will be the destiny of the faithful. One of the reasons people show up on Sunday morning is this inarticulate yearning and wishfulness for a lost communion. We are not sure how or when it was lost, but we sense the loss. Nor do we know much about reentry and access into that fellowship. There is, nonetheless, a yearning. That yearning is the hope of the congregation, and the task of the preacher is to bring to speech that deep yearning. In that speech the preacher also dares to respond from the other side; to speak for the God who has authorized and evoked the yearning, who yearns as we do for another beginning. The preaching moment occurs in the midst of this terrible loss and this resilient hope. Our speech in the context of loss and hope affirms who we are and what has been promised among us.

The sermon, and the gathering all around the sermon, invite persons into a community where communion is sought and known, celebrated and valued. We bear witness to the one who meets us in community, the one who

specifies the costs and joys of such communion. We do
more, however, than bear witness. The gathering of the
faithful embodies and enacts that communion. How awesome that our meeting might in reality be "The Meeting"!

That communion for which we yearn, which we
have lost, and might now enact, has many dimensions of
food and drink, of giving and receiving, of caring and
yielding, of deciding and singing. Most elementally in
Christian tradition and Christian practice, it is speech that
is the central act of communion. In this meeting, we listen
and answer; we are addressed and respond. We speak
with God and we speak with each other. How we speak
matters enormously, because the shape and power of
everything else in the meeting is put at risk and made
possible by our speech with each other. We may be
tempted to distorted, safe speech. Or we may settle for
silence, because faithful speech is too risky and requires
too much. Where our lives are reduced to silence, either in
fear or in indifference, communion likely does not happen. Here, through speech, as through bread and wine,
we are invited to share in the fellowship and communion
of the Holy Spirit.

Two Modes of Muteness

So who is out there? Who comes with this loss, wistfulness, and hope? We come to this meeting, I submit, as
emaciated persons. We have been reduced to silence, to
docile speech, to non-committal chatter. We have been
intimidated to speak only what is approved, what is
expected, what is safe. Because of seduction and intimi-
dation, we say much less than we know, much less than
we hurt or hope, much less than we crave to say.

Our reductionisms in speech reflect a larger reductionism about communion. There is something covenantal, mutual, risking, demanding, surprising, frightening,
and unsettling about real communion. Communion with
the holy one is nearly more than we can bear, because we

shrink from a meeting shaped by a *massive sovereignty* before which we bow, or by *suffering love* that is self-giving. We are always shocked that the massive sovereignty of God yields before us, and the suffering love of God demands so much. We can hardly endure the strange juxtaposition of sovereignty and grace: the sovereign one who is shockingly gracious, the gracious one who is stunningly sovereign. The shock of such a partner destabilizes us too much. The risk is too great, the discomfort so demanding. We much prefer to settle for a less demanding, less overwhelming meeting. Yet we are haunted by the awareness that only this overwhelming meeting gives life.

We come to the preaching moment having practiced less faithful, less satisfying communion, with lesser speech and lesser expectation. We come pitiful in our yearning, flattened in our loss, to see if there is speech and act that can take us again into communion that is genuinely blessed, communion for which we have been made, and from which we may live in freedom.

Reduced communion and reduced communication take two identifiable forms in our society. As Robert Bellah and his colleagues have shown so well, one form of reductionism is the practice of a subjective consciousness.[1] That is, we no longer imagine a real live, responding other with a center of its own. We imagine that reality is only us, our yearnings and our cravings. In such a collapsed world, there is no real speech, because there is no one but us, no one to address, no one to answer, no one to whom to speak seriously, no one who addresses us with authority. We are seduced into being alone, alone with our wishes and cravings, but also alone with our hopes and our fears, alone in our silence, without speech.

This subjective consciousness, as Alisdair MacIntyre has also shown, is manifested in both public and personal arenas.[2] In the public arena, such subjectivity is visible as a "managerial" consciousness in which all reality is reduced to problem-solving. Speech and act become only modes of instrumentalism for the satisfaction of needs and the productivity of payoffs. Absent from such speech is any practice of commitment that may raise any critical question. In the more personal arenas of our lives, an excessive "therapeutic" preoccupation may seduce us into yearning for relations in which there is no sacrifice, durability, or responsibility. This misguided passion for escaping loneliness through satiating relations leaves us even more alone. The world is defined by one's subjective shaping of reality, a shaping that can never satisfy, nor lead to communion, because the partner is permitted no real existence of his or her own.

The analysis of Bellah and his colleagues surely characterizes our seductive situation correctly. We are indeed seduced in our society into a subjective consciousness in which our public action is instrumental and our deepest yearnings are privatized and individualized. We did not rush into such a seduction. It happened to us without our noticing. Nonetheless, these are the folk who come to share in the sermon, emaciated by the loss of real speech and real reality, the absence of serious commitment, the lack of the sureness of a sovereignty outside ourselves. We come with empty self because we have eliminated the real live "Thou" who could make us persons.[3] We arrive at this moment of proclamation utterly alone, yearning for communion, having reduced life to categories that preclude communion.

There is a second form of reductionism that keeps us from communion. It is an uncritical form of objectivism about God that assigns everything to God, that empties one's own life of dignity, worth, and authority, and that imagines that everything is settled on the unchanging terms of divine sovereignty. This reduction may be a reaction against extreme subjectivism, even as subjectivism has been a response to a hard, cold, and tyrannical objectivism.[4] This second reductionism is powerful in the North American scene that lusts after a settled, uncritical religious assurance. It is evident among those who have endlessly accepted the affirmations of church faith, with all its flat moral claims. It is present among those who have returned again to such uncritical affirmation after a foray into lonely subjectivism. Such objectivism celebrates a God beyond reach, beyond question, beyond risk, beyond transformation. This God, through misconstrued notions of omnipotence, omniscience, and omnipresence, knows nothing of human need or suffering, acknowledges nothing of the brutal reality of "absence," and so sponsors a ready, cheerful, unhesitating submission.

Out of that posture, we come to worship and to the moment of speech in the midst of a world that seems fickle and unstable. We imagine we have arrived at a stability rooted in heaven. That stability, however, is such a heaviness that it crushes, it denies honor to us, and in the end does not take us seriously. Worship in such objectivism may be happy, positive, and upbeat. God seems easily available. Life is good, or is said to be good for those who gather in front of the cameras.

Such worship, however, is mistaken, dishonest, and destructive. The danger in such speech and worship is on two fronts. First, such worship is destructive because it requires persons to engage in enormous denial and pretense about how life really is. Such little islands of happiness characteristically fail to take into account the reality of evil and the depth of the crisis of theodicy.[5] There are deep justice questions in the life of each of us and in our common life, and they must be faced. Indeed, they must be faced at the throne. Or worse than the denial, the repression of the issue of injustice creates guilt. If God is so unambiguously good as this religion claims, then when there is trouble it must be my fault, whether it is a cancer diagnosis or a lost job or a fracture in the family. With squinting eyes I study how to repent so that the unquestioned goodness of God may be embraced. Such a reductionist faith can scarcely help people who have a discerning sense of the brokenness in the world or in our lives. We interpret the brokenness to be simply deep layers of guilt for all wrong. By yielding everything to the benevolence and almightiness of God, we keep alive a reductionist sense that the world will hold together—but at such cost!

Second, such happy confidence in God is dangerous because it screens out the public aspects of our life. Uncritical celebrative liturgy turns out to be an ideological legitimation for the status quo that announces that the system is working well and needs only to be honored and trusted.[6] Since it is working so well, it must be God's preferred system to be defended everywhere in the world, but especially in this community of the faithful. Thus, for example, such faith gives ideological support to the arms race.[7]

This second reductionism leaves us as those who have reduced joy to positive feelings, who have confused faith with satiation, and who believe it is better to be nice at the throne than it is to be honest, who must practice denial and guilt in order to enhance God.[8]

Our cultural context of worship and preaching, then, includes the twin temptations of an extreme subjective consciousness and an extreme objective consciousness. The subjective pole imagines there is *only me* and the world can, therefore, be mobilized around me. The objective pole imagines there is *only God* who lives as high and good as Oral Roberts says. I exist only to the extent that I submit to this great self in the sky. The first reductionism, I submit, leads to anxious *alienation,* and the second leads to a deep *rage.* The first believes that all justice questions are irrelevant because there are no real relations requiring justice. The second reductionism believes there is a norm for justice; God is always right. If God is always right, I am wrong most of the time. The rage comes because I know better, but I am required and seduced into a posture against my judgment. The two reductions intensify each other. The one invites me to exaggerate trust in my own judgment. The other requires me to disregard my own judgment for the sake of this omnipotent one.

Preaching happens in the context of those who believe, but who believe in reduced ways. There is a yearning for communion, but it is communion that has been rendered well-nigh impossible. Either there is an *exaggerated self* that gives God no access; or there is an *exaggerated God* who permits nothing of us in the transaction. Those with an exaggerated sense of self end in alienation, left all alone. Those with an exaggerated God are engaged in denial, which in the end generates rage and despair.

Such alienation and muted rage have a central characteristic in common: an absence of conversation, a loss of speech. In both cases, life is reduced to silence. Where there is theological silence, human life withers and dies. Where there is theological silence, blessed communion is impossible. In the face of that dread silence, the preacher comes to initiate, to reinitiate, to reenact speech that permits the communion for which we so deeply yearn. In an exquisite phrase, Robert Alter speaks of "the quintessential biblical notice of the nexus of speech that binds man [sic] and God."[9] It is speech and only speech that bonds God and human creatures. The preaching task is to guide people out of the alienated silence of exaggerated self, and out of the silence of denial and rage of an exaggerated God, into a serious, dangerous, subversive, covenantal conversation, a conversation that is the root form of communion. Communion is not possible where speech is destroyed either by selfishness or by submissiveness.[10] In the midst of these reductions, the preacher is invited to speak in ways that open a world of conversation, communication, and communion.

It is the preacher's task to carry on both sides of the conversation at the beginning. We are indeed speech creatures; we live by words, words spoken, words heard, words addressed and answered (cf. Deut. 8:3). It is a long-held opinion among us that it is the new, sovereign, gracious speech of God that breaks the grip of silence. The preacher is charged with speaking the word that permits new communion. It is commonly assumed that it is the speech of God that makes communion possible. That is, communion results from divine initiative. That is sometimes true. As we shall see, however, the speech of Israel can also initiate communion, when it is speech that is as bold as it is faithful.

The preacher speaks to overcome an exaggerated sense of self. The preacher voices the speech of God, which rushes into the autonomous self-sufficiency of a closed self. That speech is speech of promise and speech of demand, speech of grace and speech of sovereignty.[11] The preacher also speaks to overcome the exaggeration of God. The preacher then voices the speech of crushed human voices, persons too long engaged in denial, too long burdened with superfluous guilt, too long pent-up with rage, speech that must burst open in impolite ways in order to rush against an overstated God. Because an exaggerated God and an exaggerated self do not communicate very well, do not listen and answer very well, the preacher must take up the conversation from both sides, articulating the protest of self that then can move to praise, risking the candor that becomes the seedbed of communion.

Now I will consider the gift of speech that the texts of Israel offer us, the gift of speech that may override both reductionisms and in the end permit, practice, authorize, and enact genuine, joyous communion. I propose three dimensions of this speech. It will become clear that these three dimensions of speech follow the structure of the lament psalm,[12] but the speech patterns I will exposit are pervasive throughout Israel's tradition. Transactions between God and human persons depend on speech. Words heard and spoken are the mode of our most characteristic way of communion. Our task in life is to share in that conversation. We are all of us in some way creatures of a word. When the words stop, when the conversation ceases, we shall no longer be in communion. Consequently, we shall no longer exist. We live only as we engage in serious conversation.

Muteness Broken by Abrasiveness

The first dimension of speech in this reinitiated conversation is *the voice of the worshiper in pain, protest, and need.* The voice of the ones worshiping must be brought to speech by the preacher in all its emaciated yearning. If the community had its own voice, the preacher could attend to God's part in the conversation. In a social context where silence, docility, and passivity have become virtues, however, the community has no voice; the preacher must speak first the daring, risky words that the community does not know how to speak for itself. The preacher dares to speak the word of yearning and insistence that may force a new conversation with God. It could be that God will speak first. There are, however, ample biblical texts to suggest that it is the voice of human hurt and hope that evokes the presence and response of God.

The textual memory of Israel provides rich and passionate models for what the muted ones might say at the throne if they had tongues and courage for speech. Much of the Psalter portrays muted Israel finding its voice at the throne. Thus Israel can say:

> I was dumb and silent,
>   I held my peace to no avail;
> my distress grew worse,
>   my heart become hot within me.
> As I mused, the fire burned;
>   then I spoke with my tongue.
>
> (Ps. 39:2-3)[13]

When the muted ones in Israel begin to speak, their speech is funded by the burdens of rage, alienation, resentment, and guilt. These burdens have been reduced to silence, but now they are mobilized in their full power and energy. The psalm breaks their silence. The preacher can bring that tradition to speech and once again make it available in the present tense. When the preacher breaks the long silence that has been imposed and embraced, the preacher breaks the silence even as the psalmist has done.

As the preacher breaks the silence, so the gathered congregation notices the broken silence, notices the possibility of speech, ends the alienation, overcomes the denial,
breaks the guilt. The move is from the textual memory to
the preacher to the community. Speech resumes and life
begins afresh.

The speech asserts that we are not alone, either in
self-sufficiency or in blind submissiveness. There is a second party present to our life. The daring speech of the
preacher and the congregation addresses the one who has
long been absent, rejected, or unnoticed. The speech is
like that of a child who watches while a long-absent parent
comes home. The child is glad for the return; but the first
speech is an overriding sense of resentment because of the
absence, the silence, the disregard. The first speech is a
speech of hostility addressed to someone who matters
intensely, who has continued to matter even in the
absence. The daring of the preacher, in making use of the
old textual tradition, permits the speech of the human
community to address God, open communication, risk
address that violates religious reductions, and speak in
yearning beyond self-sufficiency and in honesty beyond
submissiveness. Something new is made possible in this
moment of protest and candor.

Israel's first speech, which may be replicated by the
preacher, is a speech of profound need and hostility. The
lament psalm offers Israel's characteristic way of opening
a new world by way of daring protest. Such first speech
may sound like this:

> How long, O Lord? Wilt thou forget me forever?
>   How long wilt thou hide thy face from me?
> How long must I bear pain in my soul,
>   and have sorrow in my heart all the day?
> How long shall my enemy be exalted over me?
>   (Ps. 13:1-2)

How long indeed. It has been very long, seemingly an
eternity. Now the speech explodes with having waited too
long. All parties are surprised at the depth of the hostility.

That hostility, however, is present both in the text and in the community. The opening speech is about God's failure and neglect in the relationship.

The alienation and the rage have long festered in the silence. Now the speech erupts in indignation and urgency. For a long time things have not been right. Finally there is speech. The speech is on the tongue of the poet. Finally comes the poet to speak the rage and resentment that will tolerate no prosaic utterance. The indignation is not resigned. It is an act of insistence and of hope:[14]

> And now, Lord, for what do I wait?
>   My hope is in thee . . .
> I am dumb, I do not open my mouth;
>   for it is thou who hast done it.
> Remove thy stroke from me;
>   I am spent by the blows of thy hand.
>   (Ps. 39:7-10)

Indignant hope is sounded because the speaker believes there is still this one to whom speech may be effectively addressed. There still is a serious conversation partner. In the very act of this speech, the world is already reshaped. It is reshaped with a chance of community and communion. It is reshaped with a possibility for dignity and self-respect. There is speaking and a passionate conviction that there is listening.

The psalms are permeated with poems like these, which are passionate in their address of God, and which speak directly to God concerning protest, pain, and need.[15]

> Turn, O Lord, save my life;
>   deliver me for the sake of thy steadfast love.
> For in death there is no remembrance of thee;
>   in Sheol who can give thee praise?
> I am weary with my moaning;
>   every night I flood my bed with tears;
> I drench my couch with my weeping.
> My eye wastes away because of grief,
>   it grows weak because of all my foes.
>   (Ps. 6:4-7)

The same poignancy of hurt and hope that abounds in the Psalter is brought to speech by the two root persons in our originary memory. Our father, Abraham, is disciplined and restrained in articulation, but nonetheless daring in his address to God. Abraham's credentials as one utterly obedient to God are in order (Gen. 18:17-19). He does not, however, shrink from his duty or his freedom as Yahweh's best friend.

Out of his friendship, Abraham daringly speaks to Yahweh as no one has ever spoken before (18:23). As Abraham and Yahweh survey the moral wreckage of Sodom, Abraham asks, "Will you destroy the righteous with the wicked?" Abraham raises new questions for Yahweh and forces Yahweh to make new decisions. Twice Abraham reminds Yahweh, "Far be it from you." That is, it is unworthy of you to act as you plan to act. Then comes Abraham's daring taunt: "Shall not the judge of all the earth do right?" Abraham reminds Yahweh that Yahweh must act in certain ways in order to be the God Yahweh intends to be.

Our other root person is Moses. In our familiar perception, Moses is the lawgiver par excellence. For our purposes, however, it is more crucial to discern that Moses is a relentless petitioner who will intimidate God and assault the throne until God's holy self-regard yields to the need of Israel. After the manner of Moses, the mute ones of Israel are invited for a moment to turn their attention away from the Commandments and to move into hope-filled, insistent prayer. Moses' prayer may model our own dangerous speech.

The prayers of Moses, which provide a text for our speech, are not deferential. Moses is insistent. He repeatedly takes bold initiative with God:

> Why hast thou dealt ill with thy servant? And why have I not found favor in thy sight, that thou dost lay the burden of all this people upon me? Did I conceive all this people? Did I bring them forth, that thou shouldst say to me, "Carry them in your bosom as a nurse carries the sucking child, to the land which

> thou diest swear to give their fathers? . . . If thou wilt
> deal thus with me, kill me at once, if I find favor in
> thy sight, that I may not see my wretchedness."
> (Num. 11:11-14; cf. Exod. 32:11-13, 31-32;
> 33:13-16; 34:8-9)

This is the voice of a man, a tradition, and a community
that was too long muted by Pharaoh. Moses and Israel
had learned that muteness leads to brick quotas. Silence
results in oppression. Now Israel has exchanged masters,
Yahweh in the place of Pharaoh (cf. Lev. 42:25). Israel
thus will not practice muteness before Yahweh as it had
done before Pharaoh. Israel had waited too long in silence
before Pharaoh. Moses will not therefore be silent before
Yahweh. Moses' prayers, and therefore Israel's speech,
preclude any seduction of self-sufficiency and any temptation to blind docility. Israel knows that muteness in the
face of power might lead to a new enslavement. Therefore
Moses petitions, intercedes, protests, cajoles, delivers
ultimatums, and plays brinkmanship. It is in the midst of
such speech, not before but only in the midst of such
speech, that Yahweh responds and yields. It is the urgent
prayer of Moses that makes new life repeatedly possible
for Israel. In Moses' daring speech, the balance of power
between heaven and earth is kept under review and, from
time to time, revised.

In all three cases of lament psalms, the urging of
Abraham, and the prayers of Moses, new conversations
are modeled that open up new saving, liberating possibilities. These possibilities could not emerge when the
human partner is mute. In the tradition of Abraham and
Moses, the preacher models for the community the speech
that belongs properly to biblical faith—speech that must
be practiced on earth toward heaven if heaven is to be
moved to care and act.[16]

The capacity to bring need and pain to public
speech is crucial for our life with God and for our life in the
world. The act of bringing the pain to public speech is at
the heart of the Exodus narrative:

> And the people of Israel groaned under their bond-
> age, and cried out for help, and their cry under bond-
> age came up to God. And God heard their groaning,
> and God remembered his covenant with Abraham,
> with Isaac, and with Jacob. And God saw the people
> of Israel, and God knew their condition.
> (Exod. 2:23-25)

On the basis of that originary narrative, the same power of
the cry of pain is found even in Israel's ethical reflection.
Moses' law echoes and reiterates the primal petition of
Israel:

> You shall not wrong a stranger or oppress him, . . .
> you shall not afflict any widow or orphan. If you do
> afflict them, and they cry out to me, I will surely hear
> their cry; and my wrath will burn, and I will kill you
> with the sword and your wives shall become widows
> and your children fatherless.
> (Exod. 22:21-24)

The cry of the helpless, if they have a voice, will mobilize
God to act.

It is the same in the presence of Jesus. Bartimaeus,
the blind man, daringly initiates interaction with Jesus.[17]
He cries out saying, "Son of David, have mercy" (Mark
10:47). Remarkably, the people around him try to silence
him, to drive him back to his muteness (v. 48). In an act of
urgent hope, however, the beggar cries out all the more.
Jesus hears. Jesus heals and concludes, "Your faith has
made you well" (v. 52). A capacity to cry out the pain has
caused health to come. The pain of the world, embodied
in the largely silent congregation of ancient Israel and in
the silence of this blind beggar, is the stuff out of which
new life comes. Newness, however, requires faith in
order to speak the pain. Out of voiced pain, Bartimaeus is
permitted a new life: "Immediately he received his sight
and followed him on the way" (v. 52). Had he not cried
out in pain, he never would have come to a new life of
discipleship.

The sermon is an invitation, a modeling, and a permit. Such speech is courageous faith which addresses God about the pain of the world. As with Bartimaeus, there are powerful forces that want to keep the pain mute. The text and the sermon, however, refuse to succumb and submit to such pressure, refuse silence and know that such speech is necessary for new life.

Life Voiced from the Other Side

In Israel's characteristic pattern of speech, the address of pain to God, evokes *God's powerful, intervening response.* God speaks and God acts. This response of God is the second element of faithful speech that becomes an evangelical theme for the speech of the preacher. Israel's speech addressed to God is filled with pain, protest, and need. The news is that Israel's speech receives attention and an answer from God. That is the wonder of evangelical faith and evangelical experience. God is not silent in response. Characteristically, God is not offended by such speech but welcomes such speech and is moved to new possibility by it.[18]

The preacher thus continues this two-way conversation by sounding the voice of God. The preacher renders the voice of God in the ongoing dramatic event of preaching. The preacher draws God freshly into the question of pain and need and mobilizes God to notice and face the question in new ways. To be sure, God's response is not *pro forma,* automatic, or predictable. As we are to practice freedom and daring in our address to God, so the preacher must acknowledge that God's response is free and open. The only conversation worth having occurs when both parties can speak in freedom and candor, because then the conversation has a chance for newness. I suggest four responses God makes to Israel's daring speech, though you may think of others:

1. The immediate answer to Abraham's daring speech (Gen. 18:28-32) is harsh and unresponsive. The

city is destroyed. Ten righteous persons could not be found to save the city. Or, as Jeremiah later concludes, not even one righteous person could be found to save the city (Jer. 5:1).

The destruction, however, is only the immediate response of Yahweh.[19] The question of Abraham lingers for Yahweh: "Shall not the judge of all the earth do right?" There is a brooding on God's part and a quite delayed response. Yahweh's ultimate response, wrought through generations of brooding, comes to speech in the pathos of God in Hosea 11:8-9. There Yahweh says:

> How can I give you up, O Abraham!
>   How can I hand you over, O Israel!
> How can I make you like Admah!
>   How can I treat you like Zeboiim!

That is, how can I enact the destruction of Sodom and Gomorrah all over again? Yahweh answers the rhetorical question: I cannot treat Israel like that. Yahweh enters into the grief of Israel and the judgment and terror evoked by Israel's conduct. In the delayed response of Hosea, the speech of Abraham has driven Yahweh to engage the pathos of Israel, and embrace that pathos as God's own. That embrace of pain rests at the center of the gospel story available to the preacher. God's response in the poem of Hosea is neither a denial of pain nor a supernatural triumph over pain. When God's long silence is broken, God is moved to new embrace. That embrace is echoed in the compassion of Jesus, for example, in the rending of his innards when he saw the pain of the world (Matt. 9:36; 11:14; 18:27).

2. Yahweh makes a very different response, however, to the assaults of Jeremiah. The complaint prayers of Jeremiah, as Baumgartner has shown, follow the standard form of prayer and response in Israel.[20] They are thus prayers both conventional in form and personal in their anguish and hope. They reflect the troubled situation of Judah drawing close to destruction and death. They are

uttered in a moment when it is urgent to evoke Yahweh's saving response.

What is startling in these prayers, is that Yahweh does not answer according to the convention of gracious intervention. Instead, Yahweh's answer is a hard-nosed insistence on obedience and repentance. It is precisely the conventional form and its violation that creates the rhetorical power and destabilization expressed in Yahweh's response:

> Therefore thus says the Lord:
> If you return, I will restore you,
> > and you shall stand before me.
> If you utter what is precious, and not what is worthless,
> > you shall be as my mouth.
> They shall turn to you,
> > but you shall not turn to them.
>
> > (Jer. 15:19)

Yahweh gives a promise of companionship and solidarity, but not release from the burden.

The response of Jer. 12:5-6 is even more harsh and insistent:

> If you have raced with men of foot, and they have wearied you,
> And if in a safe land you fall down,
> > how will you do in the jungle of the Jordan?
> For even your brothers and the house of your father,
> > even they have dealt treacherously with you;
> > they are in full cry after you;
> believe them not,
> > though they speak fair words to you.

Jeremiah does not get the answer he wanted, the answer that literary convention had promised. He does, however, receive an answer. Jeremiah is not caught in a monologue. There can be a conversation, albeit an unequal one. There is another voice and another presence in his life of lonely abandonment. There is no doubt that the voice of Yahweh is powerful to Jeremiah. There is no doubt that Jeremiah knows he must come to terms with Yahweh. At the same time, however, Jeremiah is not sure that God's voice is reliable. Indeed, Jeremiah suggests that the voice and person of God are fickle (20:7). Nonetheless, the prayer of hurt and need is not ignored or unanswered.

The reality of Yahweh's answer is a note that the preacher must speak. Conversations of serious engagement with God are not conversations in which God must always respond on our terms. But even the harsh response of God indicates that Jeremiah is taken with utmost seriousness by Yahweh. Yahweh's answers to Jeremiah articulate no easy grace but are nonetheless a gift in the face of a silent, stonewalling world. This God does not stonewall. There is a mercy, if even a severe mercy.[21]

3. The poem of Job embodies a third response that God may make to the insistent voice of faith. As you know, Job pushes his attack on God as far as a voice in Israel dare push. In chapter 9, Job asserts not only that God is unreliable, but is in fact a liar (vv. 20-22). Job never pushes to God's nonexistence, for then he would quit speaking and be reduced to silence, and Israel is never reduced to silence for long. Muteness is practical atheism. Job keeps believing and speaking; he lives for the dispute. Likely that is why in ancient Israel there are no atheists.[22] The conversation of faith is the best action in town. Job is characteristic of Jewishness that finds dispute a viable, crucial form of faith.

Job delineates his experience of negation, of God's absence and silence, of God's refusal to deal with his issues. Job yearns most for an answer, any answer, because he prefers a harsh dialogue to an empty monologue. As the poet of Job wishes to keep the dialogue going, so the preacher must voice and enact the same urgent wish against a world that wants everything reduced to a controlled monologue.

In the whirlwind speeches of chapters 38–41, Job receives all he bargained for and more.[23] Job already had sung great doxologies to God (Job 5:9-15; 9:4-10). Job knew that God must be praised. Job conceded everything about God's power. In that regard the whirlwind speeches do not advance the argument; they only echo and intensify the claims Job has already acknowledged. Rather than new substance, then, what is important is that this is a voice from the other side. This poem is not Job shadow-boxing with himself; but it is the very voice of the creator God now delineating and responding to Job's precarious position in the presence of God. The speeches of Yahweh press hard against Job's presumed world and, in the end, destabilize him.[24] Job's security is gone. His preeminence has vanished. Job is pressed by the rhetoric of God to reevaluate his place in the world, his role in creation. He is, by weight of the evidence, by the power of rhetoric, driven to awed submission.

Yahweh must state Yahweh's own preeminence and state it again and again as though Job has touched a delicate nerve. In the course of this self-announcement, Yahweh changes the subject on Job. Job's attempt to raise the issue of God's injustice is smothered in the torrent of words about God's greatness. Or as someone has said, this is a God, who when asked about justice, responds with a description of a crocodile:

> I will not keep silent concerning his limbs,
>   or his mighty strength, or his goodly frame.
> Who can strip off his outer garment?
>   Who can penetrate his double coat of mail?
> Who can open the doors of his face?
>   Round about his teeth in terror.
> His back is made of rows of shields,
>   shut up closely as with a seal.
> One is so near to another
>   that no air can come between them.
>   (Job 41:12-16)

The preacher has an awesome text in this response of God. The poem shows God answering, yet in the very act of answering, refusing to respond. The poem asserts that there can be a profound incongruity between prayer

to God and God's awesome response. God hears and
answers Job's prayer in terms of God's sovereign freedom
and self-regard. The new world in which Job must live is
a world in which God's majestic presence is at the center.
Job has been theologically displaced and marginalized.

As God asserts God's own sovereignty, God invites
Job to a proper mode of speech. Job has sung doxologies
about God (cf. 5:9-16; 9:5-12), but they are doxologies that
are in fact a disputation. Now God speaks in a disputation, but it is in fact a doxology. It is in the character of
God to be praised. God will be praised, even if the praise
must come out of God's own mouth. If Job does not ade-
quately speak praise of God, then God will complete the
required praise through God's own words.

The outcome of this strange doxological and self-
congratulatory response of Yahweh is not that Job is
crushed and reduced to silence. Instead, the magisterial
speech of Yahweh leads to an appropriate yielding (42:1-
6). Job gains enough insight and reassurance to continue
as a person of faith in a world that continues to be unjust.
Faith, if it is to survive knowingly and honestly, must live
in an unjust world. Theodicy is overridden by doxology.

In the prose ending of the Book of Job, God salutes
Job for having spoken what is "right" (42:7-8). Yahweh's
doxology is not dismissive of Job, but it requires Job to be
repositioned vis-á-vis God. Thus the poem models a conversation between cosmic injustice and awesome sovereignty. When the doxology ends, God has not dealt
frontally with the protest of Job. And indeed, God will
not. Rather Job's life is taken up in a new conversation in
which Job is taken seriously but not ultimately, for what is
ultimate is God's sovereign rule. Job learns that while the
world may not be to his liking, the world will hold at its
center, because it is God's world. The world does not rest
in Job's virtue. In the end Job is released for yielding and
submission, for trust and praise, and finally he is released
for freedom to live.

4. The fourth response of Yahweh to Israel's cry of need merits our main attention. There is a rough consensus among scholars that the harsh and desperate lament psalms of Israel evoke from Yahweh an answering speech that is not only sovereign, but also caring and transformative.[25] That response is stylized as a salvation oracle through which Yahweh becomes present to the speaker in ways that change life and circumstance. The salvation oracle begins by naming the one whom God addresses. That address is normally a phrase of endearment:

> But you, Israel, my servant
>> Jacob, whom I have chosen,
>> the offspring of Abraham, my friend,
> you whom I took from the ends of the earth,
>> and called from its farthest corners,
> saying to you, "You are my servant,
>> I have chosen you and not cast you off."
>>> (Isa. 41:8-9)

> . . . he who created you, O Jacob,
>> he who formed you, O Israel.
>>> (Isa. 43:1)

> But now hear, O Jacob my servant,
>> Israel whom I have chosen.
>>> (Isa. 44:1)

Sometimes, however, the address is a bit more pointed as in Isa. 41:14: "You worm, Jacob."

Occasionally the naming of the addressee is followed by a fuller identification of the speaker, Yahweh. That identification reviews God's past caring actions (for example, Isa. 41:9; 43:1; 44:2). These formulae affirm Yahweh's past fidelity, Israel's dependence on Yahweh in the past, and Yahweh's fidelity in giving Israel life.

The second characteristic element of the salvation oracle (which is the distinguishing mark of the speech form) is "do not fear, fear not."[26] This articulation of assurance is at the heart of the gospel. It addresses the central human issue of fear, isolation, and abandonment.

For Israel, this speech form is peculiarly appropriate to the situation of exile. It is in exile that Israel is fearful, alone, and vulnerable. This speech form, when used on the sovereign lips of Yahweh, liberates from oppression and puts an end to exile.[27] As H.J. Begrich has shown, the salvation oracle addresses the very situation about which the prayer of complaint and petition is spoken.

The third element of the salvation oracle is either an assurance or a mandate. In Second Isaiah, it is characteristically an assurance:

> I am your God;
> I will strengthen you, I will help you,
> > I will uphold you my victorious right hand.
> > > (Isa. 41:10)

> I will help you, says the Lord;
> > Your redeemer is the holy one of Israel.
> Behold, I will make of you a threshing sledge,
> > new, sharp, and having teeth.
> > > (Isa. 41:14-15)

> I have redeemed you;
> I have called you by name, you are mine.
> > (Isa. 43:1)

> For I will pour water on the thirsty land,
> > and streams on the dry ground;
> I will pour my spirit upon your descendants,
> > and my blessings on your offspring.
> > > (Isa. 44:3)

This characteristic speech in Israel assures that God acts in decisive and faithful ways. The verbs announce that God has already acted to transform the situation in which the complaint is uttered. The speech itself, making present the power, authority, and guarantee of Yahweh, already has changed everything. The speech of God makes things new! The decisive speech of Yahweh is to be uttered again by the preacher. Each time it is uttered, the community again has a chance for new life.

This speech of salvation declares and enacts Yahweh's sovereignty. It declares and enacts Yahweh's sovereignty over situations that seem out of control. This speech assures that Yahweh does indeed govern even when situations are experienced as chaos, exile, enslavement, and death. The center has wobbled, it has not seemed to hold. But it will and it does hold wherever Yahweh comes in faithful power.

Dramatically, the power of this sovereign word of assurance and presence is all the more astonishing because it is summoned, evoked, and made possible by the petition of Israel. It is Israel's "cry of absence" that makes God's speech of presence possible.[28] The sequence of lament-response from God evidences that the sovereign presence of Yahweh would be neither visible nor effective unless Israel sounded its voice of protest and hurt. If Israel had remained mute in submission and passive in pain, then Yahweh's sovereignty would not be enacted. Where there is no such compelling speech, where there is no cry of absence and oracle of presence, life withers, persons shrivel, and community becomes impossible.[29] Without this speech we grieve hopelessly and unaltered in our silence, not understanding what is happening to us, for we do not know that we must speak and listen and answer in order to live.

When that speech of God's fidelity, sovereignty, and presence is uttered again, the world is changed. The silence of God has been oppressive, but somehow we had not noticed. We imagined that we were the children of modernity: liberated, autonomous, on our own. We thought the speech of this other one had been banished and with good riddance. But the ideology of autonomy is not sufficient. It leads eventually to alienation, isolation, and rage. In our autonomous silence, we deny our true selves, created as we are, for conversation, communion, trust, and yielding.

In the salvation oracle, the speech of life is sounded from the other side. The God who has been silent is evoked back into conversation. Yahweh concedes:

For a long time I have held my peace,
    I have kept still and restrained myself;
Now I will cry out like a woman in travail,
    I will gasp and pant.
I will lay waste mountains and hills,
    And dry up all their herbage;
I will turn the rivers into islands,
    And dry up the pools.
And I will lead the blind
    in a way that they know not,
in paths that they have not known
    I will guide them.

                                              (Isa. 42:14-16)

For Zion's sake I will not keep silent,
    and for Jerusalem's sake I will not rest,
until her vindication goes forth as brightness,
    and her salvation as a burning torch.
The nations shall see your vindication,
    and all the kings your glory;
and you shall be called by a new name
    which the mouth of the Lord will give.

                                              (Isa. 62:1-2)

Yahweh, who had been silent and absent, has been urged to speech and presence by our hope-filled yet resentful candor. The life-giving conversation has begun again. The preacher boldly speaks the word of God's intervention, rescue, and transformation. The preacher does not just tell about God's faithful presence. The sermon is the moment of proclamation. In the speaking and hearing, slaveries are overcome, exiles are ended, and death is defeated. As the hurt has been given credence in the lament, so the deliverance is enacted in the very hearing of the congregation that has yearned but dared not anticipate. The words of the preacher, reenacting God's speech of assurance, run beyond the timid yearning of the congregation, run powerfully beyond, even to authentic newness.

An Answer of Glad Yielding

In the third dimension of speech that brings reduced truth to fullness, *Israel speaks again, this time in praise and celebration.* The responsive speech that Israel makes to the sovereign assurance of Yahweh is characteristically praise:[30]

> But I have trusted in thy steadfast love;
>> my heart shall rejoice in thy salvation.
> I will sing to the Lord,
>> because he has dealt bountifully with me.
>>>> (Ps. 13:5-6)

> I will tell of thy name to my brethren;
>> in the midst of the congregation I will praise thee:
> You who fear the Lord, praise him!
>> all you sons of Jacob, glorify him,
>> and stand in awe of him, all you sons of Israel . . . .
> From thee comes my praise in the great congregation;
>> my vows I will pay before those who fear him.
> The afflicted shall eat and be satisfied;
>> those who seek him shall praise the Lord!
> May your hearts live for ever!
>>>> (Ps. 22:22-23, 25-26)

> I wash my hands in innocence,
>> and go about thy altar, O Lord,
> singing aloud a song of thanksgiving,
>> and telling all they wondrous deeds.
>>>> (Ps. 26:6-7)

> Let those who desire my vindication
>> shout for joy and be glad,
>> and say evermore,
> "Great is the Lord,
>> who delights in the welfare of his servant!"
> Then my tongue shall tell of thy righteousness
>> and of thy praise all the day long.
>>>> (Ps. 35:27-28)

> Why are you cast down, O my soul,
>> and why are you disquieted within me?
> Hope in God; for I shall again praise him,
>> my help and my God.
>>>> (Ps. 43:5)

Israel's strange conversation with God has its outcome in doxology, which is the proper outcome of one's life. As Claus Westermann has seen, plea characteristically culminates in praise. Plea ends in praise because God is responsive to articulated hurt.[31] Praise happens, on the one hand, when the isolation of alienation and the denial of rage are overcome enough to permit speech. Praise happens, on the other hand, when we are freed enough to participate in our proper vocation, which is the yielding of life to God. The two-way conversation between God and Israel consists in a cry of hurt, a saving response, and answering praise. This conversation permits us to become who we are formed by God to be and yearn to become.

The act of preaching is not instruction, rational discourse, or moral suasion. It is the invitation and permit to practice a life of doxology and obedience, which properly orders the ongoing relationship of sovereign and subject, which in seasons of trust is that of parent-child, or even friend and friend (John 15:14-15).[32] The preacher is to enact doxology with and for the congregation, which may only now dare a move out of fearful muteness.

1. Israel's earliest lyrical response to the action of God was praise and thanks. Israel noticed the transformation of its life and attributed the saving inversion to the power of Yahweh. They told and retold the narrative of inversion (Exodus 14). They broke out in song that characterized the change, and they named the one who worked the change. Miriam and her sisters took timbrels and they sang:

> Sing to the Lord, for he has triumphed gloriously, the
> horse and his rider he has thrown into the sea.
>   (Exod. 15:21)[33]

Moses and the whole company of Israel echoed and joined in the song of the women:

> I will sing to the Lord, for he has triumphed gloriously;
>   the horse and his rider he has thrown into the sea.
> The Lord is my strength and my song,
>   and he has become my salvation;
> This is my God, and I will praise him,
>   my father's God, and I will exalt him.
>   (Exod. 15:1-2)

Yahweh is to be praised. What odd language: this God is my salvation and my song.[34] Yahweh is indeed to be sung. The ones who sing are those who have had their slavery ended and with it their muteness. As song breaks forth, so freedom breaks out. God is the one who permits freedom and who evokes song, because life has been turned.

A generation or so later, the action of God is again recounted in narrative (Judges 4), but the praise of God is lodged in song. Deborah echoes Miriam in singing:

> Hear O Kings; give ear, O princes;
>> to the Lord I will sing,
>> I will make melody to the Lord, the God of Israel.
>>> (Judges 5:3)

The voice of Deborah simultaneously acknowledges the surprise of Yahweh and the new social reality of the poor now saved. Yahweh is a new God freshly acknowledged. In the very moment of that affirmation, the peasants come to life. The courage, freedom, and energy to act in history, even against established power, is evoked by and allied with Deborah's doxology:

> The peasantry ceased in Israel, they ceased
>> until you rose, Deborah,
>> arose as a mother in Israel.
> When new gods were chosen,
>> then war was in the gates.
>>> (Judges 5:7-8)

The people sing because there is a new God who confounds the rulers of this age. There is also a new mother in Israel who permits these social losers to be new people—a new family of covenant. The peasants are mobilized, and life begins again. When life begins again, Israel can only sing. Singing in Israel is never "mere" religion. Praise is always an act of political reality, daring a new way in the world.

2. Doxology liberates us toward God and away from self. We affirm God's sovereign rule of creation. As we acknowledge creator, we notice creation in a new way.

Thus the psalmist understands that our praise is participation in the great praise articulated by all of creation:

> Praise the Lord!
> Praise the Lord from the heavens,
>   and praise him in the heights!
> Praise him, all his angels,
>   praise him, all his host!
> Praise him, sun and moon,
>   praise him all you shining stars!
> Praise him, you highest heavens,
>   and you waters above the heavens!
> . . . Praise the Lord from the earth,
>   you sea monsters and all deeps,
> fire and hail, snow and frost,
>   stormy wind fulfilling his command!
> Mountains and all hills,
>   fruit trees and all cedars!
> Beasts and all cattle,
>   creeping things and flying birds!
>   (Ps. 148:1-4, 7-10)[35]

As we sing, our faces are full forward to the throne. Israel
dared to imagine, however, that in the choirs of heaven as
in the earth, we cast a sideways glance. We notice the others singing with us. We do not sing alone, but are drawn
along with all the others to the throne. We notice the neighbor. Our neighbor sings with us. We sing with the neighbor. Drawn to the throne, the differences and distinctions,
threats and fears among us are now seen not to be decisive,
because we all sing the same song to the same sovereign.
Our neighbor includes the angels, stars, and sea monsters;
widows, orphans, and sojourners; princes and priests. All
are there, entering a new world, submitting to a new
regime, embracing a new common possibility.

   3. The song Israel sings is about God's overwhelming abundance:

> These all look to thee,
>   to give them their food in due season.
> When thou givest to them, they gather it up;
>   when thou openest thy hand, they are filled with
>   good things.   (Ps. 104:27-28)

> The eyes of all look to thee,
>   and thou givest them their food in due season,
> Thou openest thy hand,
>   thou satisfiest the desire of every living thing.
>   (Ps. 145:15-16)

We bask in the overflow of creation; our song enacts the overflow.[36] We discover that some of the abundance of God's generosity has been entrusted to our hand. As the singing proceeds, we begin to notice the grace of generosity emerging in our own life. When the song ends, the conversation in the choir continues. We are left with courage, freedom, and imagination, and we are given sufficient energy to care for the humanness, the humaneness, the humanization of the world. In the act of humanizing, the song of praise continues, for the creation does what the creator hopes.

4. Our song of doxology begins with Miriam, Moses, Deborah, and the liberated slaves who can only sing. Our whole history of life with God is a doxology as we sing ourselves free of Pharaoh, the Philistines, and the Canaanites. We turn our life to God and we find our life overflowing with goodness. The song does not stop. It receives new impetus along the way as God acts again and again for the sake of our life. The faithful, obedient church keeps singing all the way to the throne. We dare to imagine that even beyond our sight, the church triumphant (that means our treasured dead) are still singing at the throne. So we dare to conjure:

> Yet she on earth has union with God the
>   Three in One,
> And mystic sweet communion with those whose rest
>   is won;
> O happy ones and holy! Lord, give us grace that we,
> Like them, the meek and lowly, On high may dwell
>   with Thee.

This hymn of praise and hope is not escapist literature. It is rather the conviction that the song goes on. The praise goes on, because the "fear not" solidarity of God-with-us goes on. Israel's singing is unendingly responsive to God's unending solidarity.

Finally, it is the poet in the book of Revelation who strains the language to tell us most and best about our summons to praise.[37] In an astonishing act of poetry, the church culminates its life at the throne:

> The four living creatures, and the twenty-four elders fell down before the Lamb, each holding a harp, and with golden bowls full of incense, which are the praise of the saints; and they sang a new song, saying,
>> Worthy art thou to take the scroll and to open its seals,
>> for thou wast slain and thy blood didst ransom men for God,
>> from every tribe and tongue and people and nation,
>> and thou hast made them a kingdom and priests to our God,
>> and they shall reign on earth.
>>   (Rev. 5:8-10)

> And they sing a new song before the throne and before the four living creatures and before the elders. No one could learn that song except the hundred and forty-four thousand who had been redeemed from the earth.   (Rev. 14:3)

> And they sang the song of Moses, the servant of God and the song of the Lamb saying,
>> Great and wonderful are thy deeds,
>> O Lord God the Almighty!
>> Just and true are thy ways,
>> O King of the ages!
>> Who shall not fear and glorify thy name, O Lord?
>> For thou alone art holy,
>> All nations shall come and worship thee,
>> for thy judgments have been revealed.
>>   (Rev. 15:3-4)

> Then I heard what seemed to be the voice of a great multitude, like the sound of many waters and like the sound of mighty thunderpeals crying,

> Hallelujah! For the Lord our God the Almighty
>   reigns,
> Let us rejoice and exult and give him the glory,
> for the marriage of the Lamb has come,
> And his Bride has made herself ready.
>
> (Rev. 19:6-7)

An examination of these culminating acts of praise suggests to me that much of our study of apocalyptic has been wrong-headed. We are too analytical, when in fact apocalyptic is literature asserting that life finally ends in praise. The theme of the praise is that "the kingdom of the world has become the kingdom of our Lord and of his Christ, and he shall reign for ever and ever" (Rev. 11:15). That is all, and that is enough. The church, in an act of doxological hope, echoes this certitude of ultimate communion each time it prays the Lord's Prayer. We confess that it is to this God that belongs "kingdom and power and glory," not to Pharaoh, not to Canaan, not to Rome, not to Babylon, not to the military industrial complex, not to the rulers of this age, not to the power of fear and hatred and hunger, but to the Lord who has said "fear not."[38] Praise is an act of poetry! It is only this poetry that will crack the muteness and let life begin again.

The problems of praise in the modern world are acute and obvious.[39] Praise is difficult for those caught in reductionism. Praise becomes problematic for those who perceive life as technique, and live life as a series of problems to be solved. Our relation with God is neither a problem to be solved, nor a technique to be practiced. For children of modernity, technique and manipulation finally silence all serious conversation. For us to be summoned to and permitted in a serious conversation is awesome, transformative, and frightening. It is the gift of the text and the work of the preacher to lead the congregation past the reductions to praise, which is in fact communion.

Judged by any pragmatic norm, praise is foolishness. It has no end beyond itself. Praise is the simple act of enacting our true purpose, namely letting God be God in our life. As that happens, we take on our true human character. In the act of praise, we become the creatures whom we are meant to be; against subjectivity that produces anxiety, against technique that leaves us empty, we are now filled with life as creatures gifted by the Creator.

The preaching event is a modeling of praise, an act of lyrical articulation that breaks the muteness and shatters the deathly control in which our life is held. It is the task of the preacher to permit such praise, to summon to such praise, and to legitimate it. That task requires an enormous act of poetic imagination. Such preaching invites the congregation out of the world of alienation and repressed rage into a world changed by the coming of God. This preaching moves the congregation to amazement and to glad obedience.

A Conversation of Two Well-Spoken Voices

The preacher faces believers whose life and faith are greatly reduced—not wrong, but sadly reduced. On the one hand the reduction is to an autonomy that ends in isolation. We had come to believe in self-fulfillment and have discovered that even a "filled" life, if alone, results in an empty self. On the other hand, the reduction is a weary, resigned trust in God's justice that collides with too much dissonant data. Such trusting ones believe passionately in God's rule, all the while silently, unknowingly building an inventory of injustices where God manifestly does not rule. In either reduction, the conversation stops, either because there is no one to whom to speak (alienation), or because there is nothing we dare say (muted rage). Either way, the conversation stops and life is diminished.

The news entrusted to the preacher, however, is that we are willed and destined to a more candid, passionate, transformative conversation where our lives are given us again. That more candid, passionate, transformative conversation begins with protest. It ends in praise, the final act of our true selves. Both the beginning in protest and the culmination in praise permit us to stand finally, freely, joyously before the throne.

The dare of preaching is to open and sustain a conversation without which we cannot live; a conversation perceived among us as subversive. For some, the conversation is an ongoing reality. In our culture, however, many have life so reduced that the conversation has ended, either in an anxious silence or in a grim monologue. The sermon must be a modeling of a conversation in which all partners speak: the speech of good friends, the speech of parent and child, the speech of sovereign and subject, the speech of creator and creature. If the human voice has been reduced to silence by desperate alienation or by suppressed rage, then the voice of God alone will not evoke praise or permit transformation. The initiative for a new conversation cannot begin simply with the voice of God, for God is already eliminated in alienation or too large in suppressed rage. The new saving conversation must begin "from below" in the cry of the oppressed, the grief of emptiness, the hurt of being forgotten. Such feeble but bold efforts at the throne break the grip of alienation that is unable to speak and of muted rage that speaks dishonestly through clenched teeth. It breaks the silence, creates a place wherein God may speak, and finally insists that God must answer.

Preaching aimed at communion is an odd act. The grim, the cynical, the urbane, the docile come to the preaching, assuming that life is already settled. Along with the cynical, the urbane, and docile, there also comes someone else to the preaching. Finally comes the poet. The work of the poet is to permit a fresh conversation among those who are too modern, too buoyant, too desperate, too obedient. The preacher starts again this other conversation. The preacher must play all the parts at the outset and give voice to all the voices. Preaching is to sound the sounds of pain, protest, and need. In a quick role change, the preacher also sounds the voice of the one who stands in solidarity with a sovereign "fear not." At

the proper moment, but not too soon, the preacher
sounds the praise; with the preacher, the whole church
breaks out into lyrical praise, because the transformation
wrought through this speech is too stunning to permit
logical discourse or sober description. The whole church
joins the song. God is praised. Life begins again.

Good friends must be in conversation or the friendship will grow cold. Parent and child must be in conversation, or the relation will stagnate along the way.
Sovereign and subject must be in conversation or the
relation will become adversarial. The very metaphor of
conversation protects against alienation and rage.[40] The
act of conversation shows that lives impinge upon each
other. The impingement is mutual, for in the process of
speaking and hearing, both parties are transformed. We
are a part of that impingement, to act and to be acted
upon. The conversation impinges upon those who are
alienated and enraged, to transform them into creatures
of praise. The conversation also impinges upon the silent,
absent sovereign and draws God back into the pain and
hope of the world.[41] The conversation transforms both
parties, permitting communion. How awesome for the
preacher to be the one who acts poetically against the
silence for a new God-given possibility that impinges on
both heaven and earth!

The preacher listens to the biblical text, which is a
long-standing conversation. The preacher listens to the
life of the people, which is always an ongoing conversation, even if often reduced. The preacher does the imaginative act of rendering in words the conversation for both
parties. "Finally comes the poet." The preacher does not
simply report the old conversation between God and
Israel as though submitting an old verbatim. Rather the
preacher offers a conversation now to be imagined,
evoked, and shaped in this moment of speaking and hearing. It is words we never knew until we heard them spoken. It is speech we never before dared to utter until we
witness this daring utterance. This speaking breaks the

rage. This speaking ends the isolation. This speaking evokes the sovereign one to a new response. The preacher speaks for the community. The preacher then dares to speak for God.

This conversation in which the preacher participates becomes the matrix for new life, for rescue from silence, for liberation from other pseudo-conversations. We find again our true conversation partner. We learn again the true subject of that conversation. The miracle is that we are heard and answered at all. The answering voice of Yahweh releases a flood of feeling, words, and resolves; rage is turned to praise, isolation is turned to community, fear becomes trust, hurt permits healing, anxiety becomes adoration.

As we find our tongues, we find our identity and our vocation. Our lives are given back to us in the oddness of praise. More we could not ask than to be "lost in wonder, love and praise,"

- wonder that overrides excessive certitude,
- love that casts our fear,
- praise that turns the reduction to glad amazement.

The entire conversation is at the outset posed daringly on the tongue of the preacher who speaks for both parties: the sovereign who transforms, the subject who yields in delight. Such preaching permits a new conversation of candor, a new abandonment in doxology, and finally the reality of communion, which is our chief end. The new permits of candor, doxology, and communion depend upon the poet. By the poet, life begins afresh—only by the poet.

3

Restlessness and Greed

Obedience for Missional Imagination

Listening as Proper Human Business

Evangelical preaching takes as a central theme the will and purpose of God for creation, for humankind, and for the church. The biblical tradition asserts that God wills well-being for the world that is radical and enduring, well-being wrought through joyous obedience. God's purpose for the world, articulated in the grand themes of the saving narratives and the prophetic promises, is that the world should come to freedom, justice, and equity.

Biblical articulations of God's purpose, however, do not stay with grand themes. The will of God is more precisely articulated in quite concrete commandments that require and demand specific actions in the service of the grand vision. The dynamic of biblical faith requires that the command should always be rearticulated for specific times, places, and circumstances.[1]

The Bible and the memory of the church is a long procession of voices that claim to speak the voice of God, or that claim to be faithful interpreters of the voice of God. The address of God to Israel, echoed through so many human voices, asserts the ways of conduct that make life possible, that make available communion with God and peace with neighbor. God's address to Israel, variously mediated, is not a heavy-handed coercion, but a gift that makes wholeness possible. The command of God and its mediation are indeed a gift of God's grace; we are made privy to the foundational requirements whereby God's good will is offered to us.[2] In the moment of preaching, it is the high call of the preacher to join the long procession of human voices in the tradition: to dare to utter what can be known about the will and purpose of God, about the costs and requirements that make joy, peace, and well-being possible in the world.

It is not a surprise to church people that the preacher should speak about the will of God, even to dare to speak about command. Popular religion in our midst, however, has greatly reduced the notion of obedience, so that it has become either a virtue too much celebrated or a burden too much dreaded.

On the one hand, our distorted notions of obedience are lifeless because they are too much taken for granted, and too well known, as though the mind of God is fully exposed. Conventional notions of "God's will" understand the commands to guarantee not only the delight of God's company but also happy family, secure economy, and prosperous life. Obedience as guarantee is a misunderstanding that works for those who find life good and equitable and whole.[3] Such a distorted notion, however, does not want to probe or notice the unavoidable ambiguity present in ethical certitude or to live with the demand of God that outruns convention. On the other hand, our distorted notions of obedience are lifeless because they are discerned only as dread censure, as world-denying prohibition. The commands are therefore old-fashioned, heavy-handed, and only for those who live in fearful anxiety. For the rest, they are outmoded and superseded.[4]

The preacher may be tempted either to sound the nonnegotiability of the command, or to abridge the gospel into a therapeutic mode that requires nothing. The live command of God, however, must be spoken faithfully by the preacher against both of these distortions: command as guarantee, and command as censure—on the one hand too eagerly embraced, on the other too carelessly scuttled. In the midst of such embrace and scuttling, the commandments persist, the voice insists, and the preacher must speak.

Even when the commandments are misunderstood as guarantee or as censure, God's voice of command nonetheless continues to haunt us. We are haunted by this voice that has called us to be. The voice of command is and continues to be a sovereign voice, a voice that addresses us anew when we embrace too easily. It is a voice that addresses us persistently and relentlessly, even when we scuttle. We are haunted not only by the voice of command that seems to be at the root of our very life. We are also haunted by our yearning to be addressed, by our need to listen. We are created for listening. It is our proper business. We are made for communion, but the communion for which we are formed is not that of mindless camaraderie. It is a communion with the one who has hoped us and made us and summoned us and who waits for us. This one who is so active before us and for us and with us, is one who cares and governs.

Our life consists in coming to terms with that one. We yearn to come to terms by listening. In the Bible, obedience takes the form of listening. The obedient life is one in which Israel listens, attends to, and responds to the voice of God. The preacher, who comes late to this traditioning processing of witnesses and interpreters, operates among those who suspect that they must listen if they are to live, who yearn to listen, who dread to listen.

Listening Blocked by Disproportion

Listening, for the preacher and for the congregation, is not easy. Listening of any serious kind is difficult. Listening is more difficult if the substance is command, for such listening is the end of our self-control and our self-sufficiency. We are schooled in self-control and self-sufficiency and now God's powerful voice of command sounds, which destabilizes our favorite posture in the world.

Listening is difficult for us because the modern world is organized against serious speech, against authoritative speech, against listening, against passionate discourse that binds one to another and causes one to yield to another. The notions of self-sufficiency and autonomy that govern our consciousness make listening difficult and obedience nearly impossible.[5] Abraham Heschel has caught the problem succinctly. While we are all children of Rene Descartes who concluded that "I doubt, therefore I am," the children of the biblical tradition offer this alternative: "I am commanded, therefore I am."[6] Or we might say, "I listen, and therefore I am." The preacher, in speaking about obedience, speaks against our modern ways of knowing and controlling. The preacher, with the congregation, is set in an epistemological crisis: she must make an appeal that violates the way we think and know and believe in our culture.

In addition to our epistemology, our economics also make listening problematic. The great fact of the Western world, and therefore the circumstance of our preaching, is that we gather as restless, greedy children of disproportion, caught in an ideology of acquisitiveness.[7] That is, social goods, social access, and social power are not equally distributed. Some have too little. Some have too much. That some have too much is intimately related to the fact that some have too little. While there are economic differentiations in the Christian community, the main body of our Western church constituency consists of adherents to and benefactors of the great Western disproportion. We have too much. We have more than our share. We have what belongs to the others, and now they want it back. This economic reality among us impinges on our capacity to hear and respond when we are addressed by God's voice of command.

Our modern ways of knowing through an imagined "objectivity" and the economics of disproportion together bear upon the preaching task of voicing God's command in at least two ways. First, our disproportion makes us restless and anxious. We rest uneasily; we are troubled and threatened. We have arrived at the disproportion by our aggressive attentiveness, and we know that the maintenance of that disproportion depends on our constant attentiveness. We are incapable of rest, incapable of Sabbath, incapable of Sabbath rest that requires we relinquish the world. We arrive at the conversation of preaching fatigued, anxious, desperately in control, desperate to have more control, desperate.[8]

Second, in our restlessness, we practice greed against neighbor. In elemental ways we are greedy people, guarding what we have, seeking more, seeking advantage. We need to have our way and our truth and our life. We want to expand the region of our control and management. The power of greed to distort in the Christian community is enormous. It sets neighbor against neighbor, so that we present ourselves for worship and for preaching deeply alienated, both having hurt and being hurt. Such greed creates a profound uneasiness that makes listening very difficult.

Thus we arrive at the moment of preaching fatigued and alienated. In that condition we want to receive God's voice of command either by reducing the command to conventional rules, or by treating the command as irrelevant to a life of self-seeking and self-serving.[9]

The disproportion is an indictment of all of us together, because taken as a social unit, we all share in the disproportion. When we look closely, however, we see that the disproportion is a conflictual matter right within the congregation that listens. In that very community are the old, the young, women—minorities of various kinds who have been marginalized, reduced to silence, nullified. They are there also waiting to listen, to be addressed, likely to be isolated in the midst of restlessness, in despair in the face of greed that alienates and disenfranchises.

The congregation addressed by the preacher is thus a strange assembly. It includes those who guard the disproportion as benefactors. It also includes those who suffer from the disproportion as victims. In that strange company, preaching is a time for speaking the command, and for listening that lets us live.

The sermon is address to us that takes place in the midst of our restless, greedy disproportion. The preacher's task is to show how that disproportion destroys and finally kills. It is, moreover, the task of the preacher to articulate an alternative that makes life possible. The theme of disproportion regularly shows up in the teaching of Jesus, when he teaches about "two" in tension:

> . . . a man had two sons (Luke 15:11);
> . . . two men went up to pray (Luke 18:10);
> . . . the two brought their offering while Jesus
> watched (Luke 21:1-4).

This drama of contrast is not simply a literary device of "binary opposites." It is rather a narrative strategy to make the contrast between those who have too much and those who have too little, and to say that our listening takes place always in the midst of too little and too much.[10]

Baptismal Imagination and Obedience

Such a context for listening presses us to the summons to speak. How to speak and what to say? I speak to you as one whose lot it is to listen to many sermons in the seminary, preached by yet-to-be-formed theologians and pastors. In their yet-to-be-formed condition, seminarians largely preach sermons filled with "ought" and "must" and "should." I have found myself growing in resistance to such sermons that purport to speak God's command. I have found myself discovering that mostly I do not need more advice, but strength. I do not need new information, but the courage, freedom, and authorization to act on what I already have been given in the gospel.

Paul Ricoeur has seen as well as anyone that obedience follows imagination.[11] Our obedience will not venture far beyond or run risks beyond our imagined world. If we wish to have transformed obedience (i.e., more faithful, responsive listening), then we must be summoned to an alternative imagination, in order that we may imagine the world and ourselves differently. The link of obedience to imagination suggests that the toughness of ethics depends on poetic, artistic speech as the only speech that can evoke transformed listening. Even concerning ethics, "finally comes the poet." It is poetic invitation that holds the only chance of changed behavior, a point understood and practiced by Jesus in his parables, which had such ethical bite, but such artistic delicacy.

Ethical appeal, invitations for listening in the church, are grounded in baptism and seek to explicate baptism. Baptism is the premise of all evangelical speaking and hearing in the church. Baptism that renounces the old ways of death and embraces a new life is an act whereby we are invited and incorporated into an alternative dream about how the world will finally be. We are indeed "children of the promise." In the act of baptism we affirm that the entire world is now safely held in the promise of God. Moreover, we affirm our obedience to that newly promised world given in the gospel.

The preacher thus may establish a fresh universe of discourse in which faithful conversation is possible. That universe of discourse does not depend upon our being conservative or liberal or in agreement. It depends only upon the common acknowledgment that we are bound in covenant to the life of God as we know it in the memory of Israel and in Jesus of Nazareth.[12] That bonding incorporates us into God's life and God's work, which is "mending the world."[13] This focus on baptism is to say that preaching is grounded in liturgy, that Word has its habitat in Sacrament. But it is to say more. It is to say that all our talking and listening is out of baptism and into baptism. We are a people that is every day summoned to die "to the vainglories of the world," and to be raised to new life. This baptismal conversation concedes nothing to our modernity and its undisciplined autonomy, its unrecognized idolatry, or its cherished self-sufficiency. Ethical discourse is not possible if the conversation concedes a hearing to autonomy, idolatry, or self-sufficiency.

Baptismal imagination (that is, life imagined through the prism of baptism) is the area of ethical preaching in the church. Such a practice of imagination begins in three central affirmations about God's life in the world:

1. A risky intervention is needed to make life possible in the world, and that decisive intervention has already happened among us. Everything is made new. There had to be an intervention, or the world, and we with it, would have continued on our way to death. The intervention is not in doubt, and it was not enacted by us. The world has been changed on our behalf. The intervention that has made the world new has been wrought by God in risky and costly ways.

The church has many ways to speak about this decisive intervention. God has liberated us in the Exodus. God has caused our homecoming. God has died for us on a cross. God has loved us and loves us still. The root of ethical discourse is the reality of God's life in the world, a reality too sovereign for some, too costly for others.

God's intervention, then, is the ground of ethical conversations. Obedience is an impossible topic for those not baptized into the intervention. Indeed, I suggest that the twin distortions I have mentioned at the outset attract us because our self-perception is not ruled by the reality of God's intervention in our lives and our world. The beginning point of ethical discourse is this: "You are not your own. You were bought with a price" (1 Cor. 6:19-20). We belong to another, the one who now addresses us with command.

2. The second affirmation rooted in baptism is this: Because God will rule, the disproportion in which we live will sooner or later come to an end, because this God will

countenance no continuing disproportion. God's intent
for justice and peace in creation cannot finally be resisted.
The kingdoms of this world, the kingdoms of disproportion, will indeed become the kingdom of God and of God's
Christ (Rev. 11:15). The end of the disproportion is the
counterpoint to the new rule of God. God's rule is endlessly destabilizing for us, because we are fearful of the
end, of the disproportion, even while we sing and pray
about the coming kingdom.

The fundamental hope of the Bible is that the disproportion will be overcome. Prophetic hope is about lion
and lamb together (Isa. 11:6-9), about swords into plow-
shears and spears into pruning hooks (Mic. 4:3-4), about
new covenant in which all will know the torah and all will
be forgiven (Jer. 31:31-34), about a new shepherd king
who will do justice (Ezek. 34:11-16), about planting and
building and enjoying the produce (Isa. 65:21-22). Israel's
hope and God's promise characteristically concern a transformation of the world of disproportion.

In the coming world of God's rule there will be no
basis for aggressive restlessness. The world can be at trustful rest. In that world there is no cause for anxious greed,
for all will be shared and all will have enough. These promises constitute a deep threat to the way we have organized
the world. The very world that threatens is a world that liberates, however, for in the end, that for which we yearn is
a world free of restlessness and free of greed.

3. The third affirmation growing out of baptism is
that our lives are lodged between the risky intervention
that God has wrought and the end of the world's disproportion that God has promised. Or, if you like, our lives
are lived between the first coming and the second coming,
between the kingdom remembered and the kingdom
promised (cf. 1 Cor. 7:29-31). Questions of listening and
obedience occur in this context between the kingdom
remembered and promised, for only in this context is
there energy for an altered imagination. In this context,
the present may be perceived differently. The present

becomes a place for risk-taking, for transformed decision-making, for participation in the transformations that God is working in the earth.

Preaching about obedience thus concerns a transformed imagination. Preaching images a world that is rooted in the promises of baptism and that issues in human participation in God's transformative work. Note well, such preaching intends both to counter the distortion of obedience that knows too well the mind of God, and to overcome the distortion of command dismissed. Faithful preaching offers an alternative both to the distortion that guarantees and the distortion that scuttles. It invites us into a world that is situated between a celebrated intervention and an awaited transformation of the disproportion.

Speech about obedience in the church cannot afford to be neutral and cowardly. It is equally important, however, that our speech about ethics and obedience not be coercive and excessively didactic. To be coercive and didactic is to lead the church predictably into another skewed notion of command. That new distortion may happen to be the favorite theme of the pastor, or a denominational ideology, or the most powerful caucus, or whatever. Such coercive distortion only drives people deeper into their settled convictions. More importantly, such self-assured partisan distortions are to be avoided because they are deeply incongruous with the claim of the gospel.

The sermon is not normally the place for concrete moral admonition, because such admonition will only enhance the partisan distortion, either in agreement or disagreement, rather than feed the imagination. Nor is the sermon the place for concrete instruction about public policy. Concreteness about policy questions, which is so crucial to the church, takes place more effectively in other contexts. The sermon is the place where the church is freed to imagine what it would be like to be intentional about mission and to embrace in our imagination acts of discipleship that we are not yet ready to accept in practice.

Liturgy and proclamation precede, anticipate, and authorize our action in the world.[14] Reflection about obedience in the sermon is more effective and compelling when it is bold and imaginative, well beyond our present capacity for action. Without such daring imagination, our action will stay in the pitiful and cowardly range where we live our timid lives. The spectacular cases of liturgy and proclamation leading to action in the world can be found in the contexts of Latin America, South Africa, and Poland, and in our own case in the Civil Rights protests. In those situations, liturgy and preaching have led to daring action for the sake of God's kingdom of justice and freedom. It is the imaginative anticipation of the gospel that invites us in many ways and places out of and beyond ourselves in missional caring for God's kingdom.[15]

The ethical question in the evangelical church is "What shall we do?" (Luke 3:10, 12, 14; Acts 2:37). What shall we do with our lives while the kingdom is coming? What shall we do while we wait? The question itself is a first important step. The question requires pastoral consideration that is neither quick, simplistic, nor easy. One way of working toward the answer is to reflect on the Commandments that we take as normative for the organization of faithful human life. Such reflection, however, is enormously demanding. It is clear from the Bible itself that the Commandments are not flat, obvious rules. They require ongoing interpretation in order that present listeners may hear the commands in all their powerful and grace-filled authority.[16]

Such interpretation is the work of preaching. The preacher is not simply to announce the old solutions. The faith question now before the congregation is fresh and requires new interpretation. We are not to continue doing the same old things, as though faithful obedience is mere replication. In our baptism, we are open to doing something new. That is the raw edge of excitement to which John the Baptist brought his listeners (Luke 3:10-14). The commands of God require a new hearing and listening in

each new circumstance. The preacher will have failed in
the urgent matter of interpretation if there is a cowardly
avoidance of the new issue and new response of faith in
the present moment. The preacher will also have failed if
there is a flat closure of the commands that does not
engage in interpretation of the tradition of commandments. I submit that the task of the preacher is to show
how the Bible itself engages in interpretation about obedience, and then to invite the congregation to participate
in that open-ended interpretive task. Such participation is
harder work than simplistic obedience, but it is the kind of
work required of a church that will be faithful.

A Command against Restlessness

As models for the church on its way to obedience, I want
to offer two expository forays into the Commandments.
My interpretive starting points are the three themes I have
linked to baptism: (a) the decisive intervention already
wrought by God; (b) the end of the disproportion; and (c)
the construction of an alternative social possibility.

The initial commandments of Yahweh given to
Israel in the mouth of Moses functioned to trigger Israel's
imagination in subsequent generations. The commandment is not simply requirement or regulation, but it is an
act of dreaming and hoping and envisioning. Israel not
only asked, "What is commanded?" It also asked, "What
is possible?" Israel's law is preached, urged, hoped with
passion. This imaginative act out beyond command is now
the urgent task of faithful preaching, for imaginative interpretation continues the work begun in the text itself. The
preacher traces the interpretive moves of Israel in
response to commandment in the hope of inviting parallel
moves of interpretation in the congregation.

In presenting these explorations, I want to show
how the tradition of the Bible itself, as we move from text
to text, engages in a bold, imaginative, interpretive act.[17]
The community of faith did not live with a flat, settled

commandments, but with authoritative ongoing teaching that always required interpretation.[18]

The first commandment I will consider is "Keep the Sabbath."[19] The commandment on keeping Sabbath is a helpful place in which to begin to think about obedience because it is not, on the face of it, inflammatory or partisan in our context. Our purpose is not to arrive at a decision about contemporary Sabbath-keeping, but to pay attention to how the Bible handled the commandment in its own extended, imaginative, ethical reflection.

1. The Sabbath commandment appears in its best-known form in Exodus 20:11:

> Remember the sabbath day, to keep it holy. Six days you shall labor, and do all your work; but the seventh day is a sabbath to the Lord your God; in it you shall not do any work, you, or your son, or your daughter, your manservant, or your maidservant, or your cattle, or the sojourner who is within your gates; for in six days the Lord made heaven and earth, the sea, and all that is in them, and rested the seventh day; therefore the Lord blessed the sabbath day and hallowed it.

We shall rest because God rested on the seventh day of creation.[20] That is, the rest to which we are summoned is a rest that God initiates and in which God participates. That God rested on the seventh day means that rest is ordained into the very structure of created reality. Rest belongs to the shape of faithful life. To take such a rest is to participate in God's own rest at the end of God's work of creation. The possibility of Sabbath rest means that the world is not marked by frenzy, precariousness, threat, or restlessness. God's sovereignty is so sure that even God can ease off daily management of creation and the world will not fall apart. The world has a life of its own with some sustaining power that God has assigned to it.

2. In the other primary version of the Sabbath commandment (Deut. 5:15), the motivation for obedience is not creation, but the Exodus.

> You shall remember that you were a servant in the
> land of Egypt, and the Lord your God brought you
> out thence with a mighty hand and an outstretched
> arm; therefore the Lord your God commanded you to
> keep the sabbath day.

The act of Sabbath is an act of remembering the liberation
that permitted new life. On each Sabbath day, the Exodus
will be enacted in a remarkable way. Your servants shall
rest "like you." Hans Walter Wolff has suggested that the
Sabbath is the great equalizer, for that day is a foretaste of
the kingdom when all—great and small—are reckoned to
be exactly equal.[21] All—masters and slaves—are to engage
in this most godlike activity of being at peace.

The two motivations, creation in Exodus 20 and liberation in Deuteronomy 5, hold together the ordered life
of God and the just intent of human life. To keep Sabbath
is to engage in an activity that holds together, sacramen-
tally, the life of God at rest and the life of the world in
liberation.

3. The Sabbath commandment also finds narrative
presentation in the Bible. The cruciality of Sabbath is articulated as a major point in the manna narrative of Exodus
16. The main subject of the story is not the Sabbath but the
need for food. Israel's storytellers, however, are characteristically relentless about and attentive to the main
issues of faith, no matter what the subject of the story
seems to be. Concerning the lack of food, the narrative
gives assurance that there is bread enough from heaven;
the counter theme asserts that there will be no bread given
on Sabbath (v. 23). No bread is given on the Sabbath
because the heavenly bakeries are shut down. The food
processors are halted so that the Chief Baker can have a
day off. There will also be no bread given on the Sabbath
because gathering is work and none dare gather on the
day of Sabbath.

Fear for bread, however, drives some in Israel to
extreme measures. In order to get bread, to overcome scarcity, and to end anxiety, some in Israel violate Sabbath and

seek bread on the seventh day. They did not need to seek bread on the Sabbath, we were told. They had enough from the sixth day when a double portion was given, and that bread was adequate and good. It did not spoil or fail (v. 24). Their anxiety about scarcity, however, overrode the gift of bread and the power of the command. They thought they would die if they did not gather.

The narrative is insistent in linking the miracle of bread to the claims of Sabbath. Three times in this paragraph, the Sabbath command is reiterated. In anticipation of the Sabbath, Moses asserts, "Tomorrow is a day of solemn rest, a holy sabbath to the Lord" (v. 23). On the Sabbath day, Moses asserts, "Today is a sabbath to the Lord; today you will not find it [bread] in the field" (v. 25). After they had violated the command, Moses asserts one more time, "How long do you refuse to keep my commandments and my laws? See! The Lord has given you the sabbath" (vv. 28-29). Both food and rest from labor have been promised by God as gifts.

Even in the face of these gifts, however, some in Israel acted out of a deep restlessness and insecurity, lacking confidence in the ordered life over which God presides. How ludicrous! Some violated the free day of rest in order to get free food, because in their anxiety they did not believe free food would continue to be given. They violated the command because they would not trust God's powerful promise, even though they had six days of evidence that the promise was trustworthy.

4. Prophetic texts take up the Sabbath command and give it fresh currency. The Sabbath is a sacrament of God's reliable ordering of life. It is also the hedge of dignity to guard each person's worth and well-being. The Sabbath is a defense thrown up by the gospel to guard the weak against the strong, for the strong have such inventive ways of exploiting the weak and using that exploitation for their own well-being.

In Amos 8:4-6, the prophet gives a sociological reading of the Sabbath day:

Hear this, you who trample upon the needy,
    and bring the poor of the land to an end,
saying, "When will the new moon be over
    that we may sell grain?
And the sabbath,
    that we may offer wheat for sale,
that we may make the ephah small and the
    shekel great,
    and deal deceitfully with false balances,
that we may buy the poor for silver,
    and the needy for a pair of shoes,
    and sell the refuse of the wheat?"

The Sabbath is a day when commercial activity stops, when the routines of exploitation are brought to a halt. Amos understands the Sabbath as the day when economic exploitation does not happen. It is a gesture of protection for the poor against the rich. Amos indicts tradespeople who use the day waiting and planning and scheming, hoping to trim the edge of the day in order to get a jump on economic advantage. Even with enforced rest, there is a scheming restlessness at work, powered by greed.

Tradespeople grow impatient with the Sabbath and want to curtail it. During ostensible Sabbath rest, some in Israel are restless to get back to their exploitation. This way of abusing the Sabbath reflects the anxiety of which Jesus speaks in the Sermon on the Mount (Matt. 6:25-33). It is noteworthy that such anxiety is not lodged among the have-nots but among those who have, yet are convinced that they never have enough. Amos understands perceptively how our acquisitiveness always drives us for more.

5. Two hundred years after Amos, after return from exile, in Third Isaiah, there is a community debate about who is included in the community and who is excluded, who is permitted to worship and to belong. Apparently rules of participation were being made that excluded eunuchs. Foreigners were judged to be unqualified. Isaiah 56 counters the dominant restrictiveness.[22] The text of Isa. 56:7 asserts in words familiar to us that "My house shall be a house of prayer for all peoples,"

that is, even eunuchs and foreigners. "All peoples," however, must meet two requirements in order to participate: they must honor the covenant, and they must keep the Sabbath.

> For thus says the Lord: "To the eunuchs who keep my sabbaths, who choose the things that please me and hold fast my covenant, I will give in my house and within my walls a monument and a name better than sons and daughters; I will give them an everlasting name which shall not be cut off. And the foreigners who join themselves to the Lord, to minister to him, to love the name of the Lord, and to be his servants, every one who keeps the sabbath, and does not profane it, and holds fast my covenant—"
>
> (Isa. 56:4-6)

It is astonishing that in this community of reconstruction, a community engaged in deciding what is ethically normative and urgent, the Sabbath is identified as the crucial act of obedience that qualifies one for God's presence. Sabbath is recognized as decisive in that moment of reconstruction, because Sabbath means desisting from the frantic pursuit of securing the world on our own terms. In that ancient society, as in ours, the practice of acquisitiveness—whether of things, power, or leisure—constitutes resistance to Sabbath.

6. Finally, along the trajectory of biblical exposition of the Sabbath commandment, I mention Mark 2:23-27 and Matt. 12:9-14.[23] In the first of these, Jesus' disciples are walking through the grain field and pluck ears of corn. The vigilant and scrupulous Pharisees attack them for violation of the Sabbath. Jesus responds with his magisterial statement: "The sabbath was made for human persons and not human persons for the sabbath. So the Son of man is lord even of the sabbath." In the second text (Matt. 12:9-14), Jesus heals on the Sabbath, arguing that a sheep can be rescued on the Sabbath, and a man is worth more than a sheep. He concludes, "It is legitimate to do good on the sabbath."

These two texts show a remarkable move in the ongoing interpretive tradition. The text we have cited from Amos shows that the Sabbath was a great line of defense against exploitation, to permit the humanization of public life. In the context of Mark's Gospel, however, Sabbath practice had become so restrictive and oppressive that it worked against acts and gestures of human caring. The command that was a guard against economic destructiveness now had been distorted to sanction other kinds of communal destructiveness. Jesus returns to the core of the Sabbath tradition to assert that the purpose of Sabbath is indeed rest, from which he extrapolated healing and eating. Some of Jesus' contemporaries had distorted the Sabbath so that it became a vehicle for the very destructiveness it meant to preclude. Jesus critiques the dominant interpretive practice of those contemporaries in order to make a faithful interpretation, appropriate to the crisis of humanization in his context.

This range of biblical texts shows that the commandments are both authoritative and problematic and are taken seriously by the interpretive community, but not with unmitigated absoluteness. The trajectory of texts I have considered shows how the Bible thinks concretely about obedience. It continues to reiterate the primal commandment; it also permits that commandment to nourish its imagination so that the commandment takes on fresh ethical pertinence in each new circumstance. Faithful ethical reflection is not mere reiteration. Preaching about ethical concerns is not the mere reiteration and assertion of absolutes. It is, rather, an engagement between textual tradition and congregational situation in which new ethical discernment is permitted and new courses of action may be envisioned and authorized out of the old commandments. Ethical reflection as evidenced in these texts is not a statement of absolutism nor is it a statement of liberated autonomy. It is neither of these, but a practice of bold, disciplined interpretation in which the old command is carried in directions that Moses and his generation never envisioned.[24]

It is precisely such bold and disciplined interpretation that makes faithful obedience possible. The preacher permits, legitimates, and models interpretation that is daring, inventive, and faithful to the fresh command of God. The preacher commits acts of intellectual courage by interpreting beyond the commandment. It is only such interpretation that can resist the irrelevance of absoluteness and that can offer an alternative to the fatigued abandonment of the normative ethical tradition.

One may respond to this analysis of the Sabbath command with the judgment that Sabbath is not a live or urgent question for us. Two answers may be given to such a response. First, because the Sabbath command seems not to be an urgent question, it may be a helpful model for ethical reflection that does not immediately become disputatious and partisan. Second, one may ask, why is the Sabbath command not an urgent issue among us? Sabbath is a critique of our entire technical way of controlling human life. Ethical reflection on Sabbath concerns yielding, relinquishing, and letting go.[25] On the one hand, invitation to Sabbath calls to mind St. Augustine: "Our hearts are restless till they find their rest in thee." Thinking about Sabbath invites us into conversation about the deep restlessness that characterizes our common life—our drivenness to have control—a drivenness that invites interpersonal brutality and public policies of destructiveness. On the other hand, reflection on the Sabbath calls to mind a quotation of Northrup Frye, who observed that "imagination is to take a sabbatical from our commitments."[26] Our commitments of all kinds hold us so tightly, keep us so constrained, that we have little room for change. Sabbath is an invitation to imagine our life differently. In risking Sabbath, we discover life can be lived without the control that reduces us and leaves us fatigued.

The ethical issue voiced in the Sabbath command concerns yielding, relinquishing, and letting God reshape our lives toward healing. Those who practice self-

disciplined renunciation and those who embrace autonomy are not very good at relinquishment. Israel's sacramental day, in contrast to such renunciation and
autonomy, asserts that trustful rest, cessation, and relinquishment may break the cycles of anxiety. This torah command is a summons to let God be fully God for one day,
so that our anxiety should not devour us. Such ethical
reflection holds transformative potential both for interpersonal matters and for policy questions. Perhaps that is what
my son meant in his teenage resentment when I pressed
him too hard and he said with hostility, "Give it a rest."
Even before my son, Yahweh, through Moses, said "Give
it a rest." We are invited to give a rest to the world and our
lives, and finally even to give a rest to Yahweh.

The theological issue in the Sabbath command is
rest. The preacher's theme for those who gather is *restlessness*. Restlessness touches every aspect of our lives: economic, political, sexual, psychological, and theological.
Restlessness bespeaks a fundamental disorder in our lives,
a disorder that reflects distortion in our relation with God.
Israel's obedience concerns the reception and practice of
rest, which God gives and which God models in God's
own life. Restlessness has become so pervasive that we
take it to be normative. We know in our sanity, however,
that such unending restlessness is not normative. We
know because God rests. God is free enough to rest. God
wills God's people and God's whole creation to rest. The
good news is that restlessness is not finally ordained in
our lives. Conversely, the reality is that if we do not halt
the restlessness among us, we will destroy ourselves and
each other. The warning given in the command is a word
aimed against our presumed reality. This Sabbath commandment is the word that will give us life. The invitation
to rest is lodged in the commandment that is the truth of
God's own rest. That obedience, however, requires imagination against our greatly reduced world.

The preacher speaks out of the alternative reality of
baptism. The preacher addresses those who seek to know

and live life from their baptism. The preacher envisions and imagines life through the command of rest. As the congregation brings its life into the sphere of the command, the disbelieving, destructive restlessness may subside. Energy may be redeployed. The energy that had been used in frantic seeking of control now may be used in the delight and care for creation. The energy not now used in futile restlessness may be used in the mission of God in creation. There will be little energy for that mission while our lives are used up in frantic disobedience. The commandment and the preacher voice a different way, of fresh energy given through trustful rest.

A Command against Greed

The second command we consider concerns coveting.

> You shall not covet your neighbor's house; you shall not covet your neighbor's wife, or his manservant, or his maidservant, or his ox, or his ass, or anything that is your neighbor's.
>
> (Exod. 20:17)

This final prohibition of the Decalogue has often been misunderstood as though it referred to an inner disposition of envy and jealousy. On such a reading, the commandment does not concern behavior, but attitude. This exegesis is well established among us, but it is not correct.

Marvin Cheney has argued, and I agree, that *covet* in the Decalogue refers in principle to land tenure systems and land management policies.[27] To covet means to arrange loan credit, tax, and inheritance so that some may have land that others should rightfully possess. That is, it is the systemic economic practice of greed.[28] This destructive form of land use begins in disproportion and ends in monopoly. There is an important line of scholarship that argues that early Israel (which gives us the seed of all biblical faith) is essentially a social revolution concerning land tenure systems.[29] This charter for "egalitarianism" culminated in the commandment against coveting that

prohibits the rapacious policies of the state that characteristically monopolize law, power, and wealth. The commandment envisions an alternative form of public life. The
commandment concerns a central question in Israelite
faith: who should have what turf, according to the intent
of God. The Bible has understood, long before Karl Marx,
that the basic human issues concern land, power, and the
means of production.[30]

I want to exposit the rich and varied ways in which
Israel interpreted this commandment. In its ongoing work
of proclamation and interpretation, Israel found the basic
prohibitions useful for its articulation and practice of a
radical social vision. The coveting commandment, like the
Sabbath command, is interpreted with great imagination
and vitality.

1. Cheney has shown that the most direct commentary on the Tenth Commandment is in Micah 2:1-5, an
oracle that articulates the complaint of the small farmer
against the large, urban-based land-owning system.[31] The
prophet mounts his harsh critique in poetic terms.

It begins:

> Woe to those who devise wickedness
> and work evil on their beds . . . .
> They covet fields and seize them,
> and houses and take them away;
> They oppress a man and his house,
> a man and his inheritance.

The oracle is against scheming, rapacious land policy. The
prophetic anticipation is that those who have excessive
land will lose it.[32] They have land that is not rightfully
theirs. Yahweh's governance will not permit those with
too much to keep what is not theirs. The land belongs to
others by right of inheritance. The rapacious have it
because they have forced a disproportion, but that disproportion, gained by acts of cunning greed, cannot be sustained. Those who once had so much, who now lose it,
will say, "We are utterly ruined; He changes the portion of
my people." Micah's concludes with this ominous line:

"You will have none to cast / the line by lot / in the assembly of the Lord." The poet asserts that there will be an assembly at which new property lines will be drawn. Nobody will be admitted to the meeting to represent the interests of the land grabbers. They will have no voice in the redistribution. They will get no land in the new arrangements. The first ones will indeed become the last ones in a most concrete way. The establishment of Yahweh's will and purpose ensures equitable land distribution and convenantal social relations.

The Tenth Commandment concerns land, which equals social power. The Mosaic vision understands that greed violates Yahweh's intent and will destroy community. The commandment itself does not specify how the prohibition is to be implemented. Implementation requires repeated interpretation as the community practices bold imagination to discern how to be obedient in a particular circumstance. The prophet Micah uses the commandment to comment on a concrete social crisis in his own experience—a crisis evoked by rapacious royal policy of the urban elite.[33] Two key insights for missional obedience are implicit in the poetic oracle from Micah.

(a) The God of the Bible is foundationally concerned with social power and its proportionate distribution. There is a moral coherence to social relations that must be heeded. That moral coherence is guaranteed by Yahweh and can be disregarded and violated only at great cost and risk.

(b) This claim about God and the distribution of land is not accepted simply on the basis of revelation, but can be established in terms of social experience. Excessive land grabbing leads to death, whether in the family, in the church, in the faculty, or in Latin America.[34] In the biblical memory, the deaths of Ahab (1 Kings 21) and Ananias and Sapphira (Acts 5) are paradigmatic examples of this powerful and demanding insight.

2. Whereas Micah 2:1-5 is a negative assertion, Israel's theological conviction about the land is asserted positively in the great social vision of Leviticus 25, the text

on the Jubilee year. A number of scholars now argue that
this text provides the cornerstone for Israel's ethical practice. The text asserts that at the end of forty-nine years,
land is to be returned to its owners, and all debts are to be
cancelled.

> In this year of jubilee each of you shall return to his
> property. . . . In all the country you possess, you
> shall grant a redemption of the land. If your brother
> becomes poor, and sells part of his property, then his
> next of kin shall come and redeem what his brother
> has sold . . . in the jubilee it shall be released, and he
> shall return to his property. . . . And if your brother
> becomes poor, and cannot maintain himself with
> you; you shall maintain him, as a stranger and a
> sojourner he shall live with you . . . . And if your
> brother becomes poor beside you, and sells himself to
> you, you shall not make him serve as a slave.
> (Lev. 25:13, 24, 25, 28, 35, 39)

The Jubilee precludes any exploitative economic practice
that is ultimately demeaning of human persons and destructive of human community. The commandment of the
Jubilee subverts most conventional economic assumptions
and practices of the free-market system, which imagines
that market power and financial leverage may operate
unchecked and undisciplined.

In any discussion of Leviticus 25, someone is sure
to assert in the guise of a question, "There is no evidence,
is there, that Israel ever practiced this program?" The
intent of such a rhetorical question is to assert that the
Jubilee provision is utterly unworkable and unrealistic,
and that Israel recognized its impracticability from the
beginning. Such a self-serving protest misses the point of
such a text. What I judge to be important about this text is
that Israel thought this provision, asserted it, hoped it.
Israel included this provision in the Torah that gives Israel
its fundamental identity. The Jubilee provision is waiting
to be implemented, as is true of many other visionary
elements of the Bible.

What a vision of social reality! At the basis of this
ethical urging is an assumption about social *entitlements:*

that members of society are inalienably assigned land, property, place, dignity, and worth that is guaranteed in the very fabric of society. One does not have to earn land or deserve it; one does not need to be wise enough or strong enough to defend it. It is simply one's right. The Bible is not naive. It knows about all kinds of calculating social practice. It knows about the rapacious taxing power of the state, which benefits some at the expense of others. It knows about the great economic combines that can crush some so easily. It knows about sharp lawyers who use knowledge for certain class interests. In the face of all those social realities and the resulting destructive manipulation, however, the Bible also knows that the fabric of society must be guarded and legitimated to protect the weak from the strong. It dares to assign that protecting function to Yahweh, who has a special propensity to guard the rights of the weak.

The text of Leviticus 25 asserts both Yahweh's radical intention and the radical social practice of entitlement that necessarily accompanies Yahweh's intention. Since the exodus, the Israelites have belonged to Yahweh, the God of freedom and justice. For that reason, Israel is uncompromisingly committed to a social practice that is congruent with Yahweh (Lev. 25:42). The text dares to assert that the land belongs to Yahweh (v. 23). It must not be sold or managed as though it belonged to anyone else, or as though it could be managed according to any other social vision. To covet the land of a defenseless person is to covet land that belongs to Yahweh, which Yahweh is free to assign as Yahweh chooses. The Bible regards moving land boundaries as a serious offense, because such movement violates the humane mapping of society that Yahweh intends and sustains (Deut. 19:14; Prov. 22:28; 23:10).

Debts serve as a form of social power whereby some remain hopelessly in bondage to others. Israel understood the powerful dehumanizing tendency of a credit society (cf. Deut. 15:1-18). The great saving event of forgiveness is debt cancellation whereby the poor are permitted to reenter the

public life of this community as respected participants.[35]
Leviticus 25 presents forgiveness as God's massive program of social healing that concerns economic debts that
Yahweh either pays or voids.[36] One of the great ethical
questions facing the church is debts and credit—who owes
what to whom and how it should be adjudicated.

A concrete embodiment of the Jubilee commandment was evidenced in a rural church in Iowa during the
"farm crisis." The banker in the town held mortgages on
many farms. The banker and the farmers belonged to the
same church. The banker could have foreclosed. He did
not because, he said, "These are my neighbors and I want
to live here a long time." He extended the loans and did
not collect the interest that was rightly his. The pastor
concluded, "He was practicing the law of the Jubilee year,
and he did not even know it." The pastor might also have
noted that the reason the banker could take such action is
that his bank was a rare exception. It was locally and inde-
pendently owned, not controlled by a larger Chicago
banking system.

Local ownership of banks is one aspect of resistance
to the threat of urban, elite power, in the contemporary
world as in the ancient world. The provision for the return
of inalienable property in the Jubilee commandment is the
positive counterpart of the commandment on coveting.
The Jubilee provision counteracts coveting and reverses its
destructive effects.

3. There is wide agreement that in the post-exilic
period the marginal poetic voice of Third Isaiah spoke for
disenfranchised priests who picked up the memory of the
Jubilee year as a source of social action and social hope.[37]
The poetry speaks in words that are familiar to us:

> The spirit of the Lord God is upon me
> > because he has anointed me
> to bring good tidings to the afflicted,
> > he has sent me to bind up the brokenhearted,
> to proclaim liberty to the captives,
> > the opening of prison to those who are bound,

to proclaim the year of the Lord's favor
    And the day of vengeance of our God
to comfort all who mourn . . . .

(Isa. 61:1-2)

The primary link between Isaiah 61 and Leviticus 25 is "the year of Yahweh's graciousness," also called "the day of vengeance"; that is, the day when God gets things right. That is the day when the weak are given their share now held by the strong. That day is a counter to coveting. That Isaiah 61 derives from Leviticus 25 is supported by the notion of liberty to captives and the opening of prison; in the ancient world (even as now) the primary reason for prison was to contain poor people who are locked up for indebtedness.[38] Cancellation of debts permits reentry into public life with dignity and freedom. The Jubilee year is the intervention of God, who breaks the vicious cycle— indebtedness and poverty—which is kept going by inhumane practices of land, taxes, and debts.[39] In this commandment, we see life without the poison of coveting and acquisitiveness.

4. Isaiah 61 (rooted In Leviticus 25) becomes the programmatic statement of Jesus in Luke:

The spirit of the Lord is upon me
    because he has anointed me
    to preach good news to the poor.
He has sent me to proclaim release to the captives,
    and recovery of sight to the blind,
    to set at liberty those who are oppressed,
    to proclaim the acceptable year of the Lord.

(Luke 4:18-19)

Michael Crosby, Sharon Ringe, and others make a formidable argument that Jesus, and especially Jesus in Luke, is implementing the Jubilee year.[40] Both the Beatitudes and the Lord's Prayer are essentially reflections of Jesus' commitment to the cancellation of debts, the return of turf, and the restoration of people to public life. The memory and vision of the church continue to celebrate this glorious, dangerous agenda.

Jubilee is the opposite of coveting. While coveting
will lead to death, Jubilee will lead to life. The giving up of
the disproportion feels scary to us, but it is, nonetheless,
the road to life (cf. Mark 10:17-22).

5. Finally, I mention the parable of Jesus in Luke
12:13-21. Two brothers went Jesus to act as probate judge
and settle a disputed question of land inheritance. Anyone
who has lived in a rural community knows that questions
of disputed land are the toughest cases. Jesus is very clear
about his role. He is a teacher and not a probate judge.
Instead of settling the dispute, he tells a story. He tells of
a man whose creed was "more." More barns, more eating
and drinking. More leisure-time activity. This creed cost
him his life. The parable invites faithfulness as an alternative to coveting.

What if the central claim of the Tenth Commandment is true: that coveting kills, that taking what belongs
to another destroys, and that life-giving social practice
requires giving things back to people! The probability that
this evangelical claim *is* true gives an urgency to missional
imagination in the church. We have, in our reductionism,
learned to imagine the world as closed and beyond transformation. We imagine the world void of missional possibility. Against such a frozenness, ethical discourse in the
Bible imagines the world in terms of mission: God's mission and our derivative ethical mission.

The theological issue related to the land is *sharing* —
respecting the entitlement of others. The preacher's theme
for those who gather is *greed*. Greed touches every aspect
of our lives: economic, political, sexual, psychological, and
theological. Greed bespeaks a fundamental disorder in our
lives, a disorder that reflects distortion in our relation with
God. Israel's covenantal obedience concerns the truth of
entitlement, acceptance of a fair share, respect for the
neighbor's right, all of which God legitimates and practices.
Greed has become so pervasive that we take it to be normative. But we know greed that kills is not normative. We
know because God does not practice greed toward us nor

toward the world (cf. Ps. 50:9-13). We know because God has given God's own self for us (2 Cor. 8:9; Phil. 2:4-11). The good news is that greed is not finally ordained in our lives. The reality is that if we do not halt the greed, we will destroy ourselves and each other. The uncompromising prohibition against coveting is a word against our presumed reality. The commandment against coveting is a word that will give us life. Our invitation to share is lodged in the commandment that is the truth of God's self-giving and refusal to seize us. But that obedience requires imagination against our greatly reduced world.

Poetic Permits for Obedience

I have attempted to exposit two commandments: "Keep the Sabbath. Do not covet." I am confident that a similar trajectory of reflection can be articulated with each of the other commandments. I am aware that I have not commented on abortion, homosexuality, disarmament, or any of the great issues before us. Finally, however, comes the poet, not the moralist. It is the poet who tries to penetrate to the underneath commitments that shape, permit, and require obedience. These two commandments converge in *the invitation to yield.* Sabbath is the practice of letting life rest safely in God's hand.[41] Not to covet is to live by the gifts given without yearning for more. To violate Sabbath and to covet is, in each case, to seize control of one's own life. Such seizing leads to death. Jesus sums it up: "Those who keep their lives will lose them; Those who lose their lives for the Gospel will save them" (Mark 8:35).

Keeping kills. Relinquishing heals. This mode of ethical reflection overrides our usual ideological posturing. The dominant ideology of our culture urges that we must be restless or we will not get ahead and we will not be safe. It requires the interpretive courage of the church, the awesome assertion of baptism, and the imagination of the preacher to evoke a world not governed by such restlessness. Our ideological posturing suggests that we must

be greedy, or we will not have enough and we will not be
secure. It requires interpretive courage on the part of the
church, the evangelical scandal of baptism, and the imagination of the preacher to evoke a world not governed by
greed. Restlessness and greed are normative ways in the
world but they are acts of unfaith. It is given to us in the
gospel to know that another way is possible and man-
dated, both in the public arena and in our closer lives.
That other evangelical way requires bold, poetic articulation to have any claim against the power of a deathly
ideology that inundates us. Such discussion of obedience
is possible when we begin to ask about the shape and
meaning of our lives.

The promises of this tradition of commandment are
finally authorized by the very life of Jesus. We may follow
Paul's lead and take Phil. 2:1-11 as a clue text for the linkage between ethical radicalness and the life of Jesus. In
that doxological text, the life of Jesus is presented in its
full, dramatic power as a life of yielding and of gift. Jesus
is the one who yielded in trust and obedience. He had all
things given to him, but he did not grasp. He did not covet
power for himself. Indeed, he did the very opposite. He
emptied himself instead of seeking greater fullness. He
emptied himself in great risk and at great cost (vv. 6-8). In
response to his obedient emptying, God gives to him gifts:
power for life, authority in the world, entry to the very
rule of God (vv. 9-11). Following the way of the early
church, Paul must resort to lyrical articulation to speak of
Jesus' gift, because there is no other adequate way to
speak. Paul finally must offer poetry that bespeaks a reality the world cannot contain.

From that lyrical outpouring, Paul leads the church
to think of its own ethical radicalness. The church at Phil-
ippi was beset, as are we, with restlessness and greed that
created hostility and division. Paul urges the church to
look·beyond such divisive, self-serving interests—to abandon the greed and the restlessness. The ground for his
argument is appeal to the dramatic story of Jesus: "Have

this mind among you which you have in Christ Jesus." Hard ethical requirement is based in lyrical affirmation. Paul's strategy, and the one urged here, is to break the frozenness and fear of the baptized community by poetic vision. That vision proposes another way for the world, a way of emptiness and fullness that is against our desperate futile seeking for fullness. Paul's intent is that the poetic scenario will energize and authorize the church to act against the dominant modes of society, modes that were surely prosaic in their rendering and hopeless in their substance.

At the end of the day, when the congregation departs, we will mostly still be children, practitioners, and benefactors of the disproportion. Some will still have too much and be paralyzed. Some will still have too little and be fated. We do not quickly divest ourselves. But the question will have been put. Can restlessness satisfy? Can greed secure? An invitation will have been issued. Return to the command, to the God who rests and gives rest, who sets free and satisfies. An alternative will have been offered. A world of God's governance ends our weariness and satisfies our longing. Obedience is the daily task of yielding more regions of our life to God's sovereign purpose. We do not yield easily. But this tradition makes clear that if we do not yield, we shall die.

The event of preaching is an event in transformed imagination. Poets, in the moment of preaching, are permitted to perceive and voice the world differently, to dare a new phrase, a new picture, a fresh juxtaposition of matters long known. Poets are authorized to invite a new conversation, with new voices sounded, new hearings possible. The new conversation may end in freedom to trust and courage to relinquish. The new conversation, on which our very lives depend, requires a poet and not a moralist.[42] Because finally church people are like other people; we are not changed by new rules. The deep places in our lives—places of resistance and embrace—are not ultimately reached by instruction. Those places of resistance and embrace are reached only by stories, by images, metaphors, and phrases that line out the world differently, apart from our fear and hurt. The reflection that comes from the poet requires playfulness, imagination, and interpretation.[43] The new conversation allows for ambiguity, probe, and daring hunch. It is only free people, in contexts of trust, who are able to walk close to the scandal, to be seen in its presence, to live by its gifts.

The mandate of biblical obedience begins in command. The ongoing work of obedience, however, does not end there. It proceeds by the long, continued voice of poets who dare against convention and who shatter normalcy. The command on Sabbath is clear. Its continued vitality, however, is carried by poets who imagine an inclusion of outsiders who want rest, and by a rabbi who voices the dynamic of man and Sabbath, Sabbath and woman, Sabbath and humankind. The command on coveting is clear. Its continued authority, however, is voiced by a poet who speaks about opened prisons and a rabbi who tells a story about a man who died in his greedy affluence.

Sabbath is a foretaste of kingdom. Sharing and having enough are like God's feast.[44] New metaphors permit new deeds of obedience. The poet invites relinquishment and embrace. The poet invites the listener to die to self and envisions a newness when strangely raised to new life. The issues of such transformation of imagination are not petty, narrow, or trivial. They concern having gained the world and having lost our very life in the process. The preaching enterprise concerns a freshly given possibility that our lives may be given to us again. So much of that possibility waits eagerly on the lips of preachers, the ones with "the tongues of those who are taught" (Isa. 50:4). They are the ones who invite, imagine, and interpret, who offer a hearing that is glad obedience. Such hearing and obeying depends upon the poet. Such obedience is improbable until a poet speaks among us. The church has been repeatedly obedient, but only when the poet finally comes.

4

Resistance and Relinquishment

A Permit for Freedom

Forgiveness, communion, obedience—these are the themes we have thus far explored. Each of these themes witnesses to the character of God:

- the God who resolves the residue of ache after reparations are made;
- the God who speaks a word of fidelity and assurance, breaking the cycles of alienation and rage;
- the God who commands, in whose obedience is new life.

Through these themes, the preacher gives voice to the reality of God whose purpose and character transform life. The preacher speaks of the God who is not contained in any of our convenient reductionisms, whose freedom and fidelity outdistance our categories of reason and administration.

As John Calvin understood, speech about God's character and purpose has implicit within it speech about human personhood as well.[1] Thus our preceding theological probes have implied evangelical affirmations about human personhood. The human person is:

111

- the creature who is finally and fully forgiven;
- the one who is invited to communion beyond resistance;
- the one who is summoned to obedience and life-giving listening.

Testimony to the reality of God is thus also a celebrative assertion of human personhood.

I am now prepared to focus explicitly on the evangelical character of human personhood.

In the end, all the themes I have considered concern the possibility of being "new creation," "new creature," wrought by the gospel. Human persons are creatures, created and recreated, claimed and reclaimed, according to the power of the gospel. The actual preaching situation concerns the text made available to listening persons who are in a struggle with their very identity and personhood.

In this concluding exploration, I seek to draw all of the foregoing themes together around the crisis of human personhood, because it is that crisis that is our daily, immediate, and inescapable preoccupation. Moreover, the several reductions I have explicated are decisively reductions of human personhood, human prospect, and human possibility. The human person is, by these several reductions, talked out of self, robbed of the power, courage, energy, and freedom for selfhood. It is ominous enough that the deathly ideologies in our culture are devoted to the destruction of selfhood. It is untenable that biblical faith, in its several distortions, should unwittingly be an ally in the destruction of human personhood.

In the face of such an unwitting alliance of distorted faith with deathly ideology, the preacher speaks new possibilities for those who listen. It is the task of preaching to permit the reappearance of a faithful self. That self is evoked, authorized, permitted, and legitimated in an act of evangelical imagination that posits the self outside the ideology and outside the reductionism.

The preacher provides the occasion and the material through which the self is freshly offered and freshly received. The preacher mediates what is true about us as it is known and sounded in the text. It is in the reality of being loved and reloved, treasured, trusted, summoned, and gifted, that we become free enough to be the children of God—freed for life with God.

In the texts I consider here, I will take up two models of transformed humanness, made possible by the inscrutable action of the holy God. These models provide materials out of which the listener can receive the gifts that make self again possible. Short of this news, we remain alienated, weary, isolated, and dysfunctional. Persons in such circumstances of diminishment, where the sounds of possibility are silenced, have little will or zeal for the vocation of God's trusted creatures. We need and must have the poet to affirm and enact for us our true identity and the full promise of our life with God.

Texts Hoping beyond Convention

I shall consider two texts from Daniel in relation to the theme of personhood. In these texts, we watch and listen while the power of the gospel permits the emergence of faithful selves in contexts where such selves were not anticipated. Thus the concrete texts function as case studies of the large chance of respeaking the truth of biblical faith in concrete and poetic ways.

I have chosen these Daniel texts for two reasons. First, these texts from Daniel constitute a literature of hope to sustain persons in faith, confidence, and resistance in the midst of persecution. The texts clearly deal with the public crisis of Jewish persecution under Antiochus. Through the person of Daniel, however, that great public crisis is told as a story that concerns individuals and their response of faith to the public crisis. Persecution concerns the resolve of the community of faith; it equally poses the problem of personhood and identity in an acute and urgent way. Individual persons are able to withstand the pressure of persecution and its depersonalization because they have an identity that is beyond the reach of the persecutor.[2] In the case of Israel, that liberating identity is given by God, so that persons of faith need not believe or accept the identity that their persecutors want to give them.

The strategy of the Daniel narrative, as a way of encouraging resistance and courage, is to focus on the individual person; in an individual person one can see played out most vividly the crisis of identity, the cost and the gain of having an identity beyond the reach of the persecutors. The narrative boldly enacts how and why and in what way persons of faith stand by their faith and in their faith in the face of assault.

In our own cultural context, our crisis of identity concerns not persecution, but seduction into false notions of self. The theological issue of persons in our society, however, is not unlike the situation offered in the Daniel narratives. In both situations, the invitation to an alternative sense of self depends on an alternative articulation, by the storyteller, by the poet, by the preacher. The Daniel stories, then, model an alternative personal identity that was crucial in that ancient persecution and is crucial in our contemporary seduction. In the use of these stories, the preacher works at the same task that concerned the narrator.

The second reason for focusing on the Daniel narratives is because of the literary nature of the texts. The texts are classified as apocalyptic. Such a label invites us to notice their daring, imaginative, poetic character. The rhetoric and imagery of these narratives refuses to abide by the rationality of dominant society; refuses to live in the understandable world of common sense or of common experience.[3] The rhetoric of the narrative invites the listener out beyond the world of predictability into another world of thought and risk and gift, a world in which the unexpected happens, in which connections surprise us, and in which new life is miraculously given. The purpose and intent of these narratives is to break life open beyond our prosaic reductions, to subvert our domesticated expectations, and to evoke fresh dimensions of identity and faith.

These texts invite us to imagine ourselves afresh, to embrace fresh forms of obedience, and to enjoy fresh forms of freedom. The human question is transformed in Daniel into a question of dangerous hope and daring resistance. The issue for contemporary humanness is the same as it was for threatened Jewishness in the time of the Seleucids. The issue of personhood is one of hope in the face of the powers of despair and defeat. This hope to which the text of Daniel invites us is a deep resolve to hold to a God-given identity, vocation, and destiny.[4] It is clear that we shall have fresh forms of personhood only when the poet comes to invite us beyond our reduced slaves.

Resistance beyond Docility

Daniel 1 tells a tale about courage in the face of imperial pressure and seduction.[5] I take up this text because it models an alternative mode of humanness in the face of ideological pressure to conformity. The model of humanness most readily available to Daniel and his three friends in this narrative was the route of *success through conformity*. "Go along and get along." Daniel, however, did not go along, did not conform. The narrative proposes that Jews under threat do not conform for the sake of well-being.[6] Do not conform! The issue is not different for us, with the pressure to conform to rigorous morality, liberal ideology, consumer expectations, secular competence. There is, so the text asserts, another way in the world, even in the world of Nebuchadnezzar.

The beginning of the story is in exile (vv. 1-2). The arena for faithfulness, so the story goes, is hated, feared Babylon.[7] Exile is the place where decisions about humanness (that is, faithfulness) must be made. Humanness is decided in an alien context, in the face of the empire. The narrative knows more, however, about the context. The apparent lord of exile is Nebuchadnezzar. It is nonetheless

Yahweh who gave king, temple, and temple vessels into the hand of Nebuchadnezzar (v. 2).[8] The introduction to the story reminds us that deportation of Jews has not eliminated Yahweh as a key player in their lives. Faith is possible in exile because the subject of Jewish faith, the one whom Jews trust, is the instigator of the exile. That hidden governance is not known to Nebuchadnezzar. It is known, however, to the narrator and to the Jews who heard the tale. Daniel and his friends knew something of this hidden governance, and that hidden reality redefined their character and their ability to act.

Daniel 1 is constructed in three scenes. The *first scene* presents the king's invitation to the new arrivees (vv. 3-7). There is nothing malicious or devious in the king's proposal, but it is a subtle royal seduction. The king authorizes his chief eunuch, Ashpenaz, to bring the best of the Jews into court service (v. 3). In some quarters his decree must have been seen as an act of generosity, offering upward mobility for Jewish boys. Here is a chance to make good on imperial terms.

The recruits in training are to be youths without blemish, handsome, skillful in all wisdom, endowed with knowledge, understanding, learning, competent to serve in the king's palace, to teach them the letters and language of the Chaldeans (v. 4). This is indeed "the best and the brightest"! They are the ones sought by every major college and university; they are pursued after graduation by large corporations. In the church they become media stars, and in every dimension of life they are well-connected, much sought after, well cared for, pampered, and valued.

The king proposes a three-year training program before their time of service begins (v. 5). The prospect of royal service is worth the discipline and waiting, for a good career in civil service is guaranteed. In the meantime, the trainees are to be fed at the training table with the best the empire would offer, the same rich food and wine consumed by the king himself. How seductive. How subtle. Not a word is spoken about conformity. Three years to learn the proper appetites and expectations; three years to develop admiration for the company and loyalty to its system of pay-offs. The ones who will rise in the company are the ones who will leave their private scruples and their sectarian dissent outside the door.

The royal recipe for well-being is only a recasting of the old theology of Deuteronomy. It is the same system as at home, only now it is practiced in secular, imperial modes: good people prosper. The "others" may not suffer, but they will not have rich food and will never make it to court. The narrative seems so routine. The conformity sought by the empire is not blatant, coercive, or affrontive. For any son of a displaced father and mother, the opportunity is "a more excellent way." Because of the attractive possibility of royal service, we might not have noticed the high cost of conformity.

Daniel noticed, however. The text moves us to the *second scene* (vv. 8-16) in this way: "But Daniel resolved" (v. 8)! Daniel had amazing energy to discern and decide differently. Daniel had not let the contours of his life be submerged in the conventional definitions of the day. Daniel had maintained a capacity for alternative perception and therefore alternative action. He had remained a free man, even in the hard-nosed training program.[9] Daniel's resolve creates an abrasion in the story, one not anticipated by the chief eunuch or by us. Daniel will not fit into royal expectation. He will not submerge himself in the imperial landscape. Daniel will risk his oddness.

Daniel will not let himself be "defiled" (v. 8). The use of the verb *defile* escalates the stakes of the confrontation. It contains a first hint of a pejorative comment against the empire. Daniel reckons that the imperial diet will make him unacceptable and distort his person. How peculiar! It is peculiar that marginal people should find royal food objectional, when they have a chance to abate their hunger with it. Normally it is the well-off who will disdain the diet of the marginal. Daniel, however, has his

own criteria. He does not enunciate his criteria, but they
obviously owe nothing to Babylonian reality.

Daniel's objection to rich imperial food is grounded
in the religious scruple of Jewish purity. In the Babylonian
Empire, no one cared about such an odd notion of purity.
The story reminds us that pragmatic considerations not-
withstanding, ritual purity is not a small matter to Daniel,
or to the exilic community he represents. Daniel refuses
the offer of imperial food carefully and judiciously. He
does not flaunt his defiance, but reviews his decision with
the chief eunuch (v. 6). For all his discreteness and delib-
erateness, however, Daniel acts freely and is prepared for
the risks entailed in his free action.

Daniel is not the only one to whom resistance to
conformity matters. In verse 9 we are told: "God gave
favor and compassion to Daniel (*ḥesed and raḥamîm*)." God
attends to Daniel's resolve to resist. God has been absent
in the first scene (vv. 3-7), for that scene had featured only
the royal enterprise and plan. When God's own people are
at risk, however, God becomes powerfully present in the
narrative. God intervenes quietly and indirectly, but nonetheless decisively. It is as though Daniel's great courage
has evoked God's solidarity.

As a result of God's intervention, the chief eunuch
is sympathetic to Daniel's suggestion. He hesitates, however, out of fear for his personal security, not out of any
zealous commitment to royal ideology. He provides a
marked contrast to Daniel. The chief eunuch will conform
to the empire for the sake of saving himself. Daniel will
resist the empire for the sake of saving his self. Daniel
knows that he needs to risk his life if he is to have a life.
Jesus' words on evangelical personhood give voice to
Daniel's knowledge: "For whoever would save his life will
lose it; and whoever loses his life for my sake and the
gospel's will save it" (Mark 8:35).

Daniel devises a plan whereby he can resist the
empire and minimize the risk of exposure for the chief
eunuch. Daniel and his three colleagues have ten days of

vegetables and water; the others, the control group that does not resist, have ten days of rich food and wine, ten days of conformity and accommodation versus ten days of self-assertion, self-respect, and freedom. For all parties these are ten days of waiting, ten days of God's steadfast love and mercy. Then comes the verdict:

> At the end of ten days it was seen that they were better in appearance and fatter in flesh than all the youths who ate the king's rich food.
>
> (Dan. 1:15)

We should have known it would turn out this way. It works to be Jewish! It works to resist the empire. We should have known, but we did not know. We did not know because each telling of the story draws us once again into the suspense. We did not know because each act of resistance carries its own risk and one never knows beforehand. As each act is a risk, each telling is a risk and we must await the outcome. Who knows in advance if Jewish vegetables outwork Babylonian beef? We did not know the outcome for political reasons. In our practice of poetry, however, we also did not know for artistic reasons. The narrative makes us wait. Ten days, and then the head of the chief eunuch is safe and Daniel is no longer pressured to conform. Daniel did not succumb to imperial food. The test is past. God silently guards God's own, unnoticed except by the narrator. God's silent protection creates a place in which Daniel can act out his courageous faith. Thus the narrator skillfully connects the courage of Daniel and the protection of Yahweh. One is visible and the other is hidden in the narrative; together they act out a mutuality that permits daring personhood.

This second scene, then, gives us a glimpse behind the imperial veneer of control. We see the freedom and resistance that comes from gospel-shaped personhood. Such a person as Daniel cannot be programmed by or for the empire.

In the *third scene*, we have the denouement of the main narrative (vv. 17-20). The youths have completed their training and are brought before the king. They are to be examined according to the standards Nebuchadnezzar established at the time of recruitment (v. 4). Daniel and his friends receive the highest marks and therefore the best ranking. There is none like Daniel and his friends (v. 19), not in the entire empire (v. 19). Daniel has wisdom and understanding. Indeed, they are ten times better than all the other technicians in the empire (v. 20)! Daniel confounded the wisdom of the empire, even as Joseph had done so long before him. Daniel is set for a brilliant career.

The success of Daniel is not simply the result of rigorous training or proper diet. It is a gift of God. God is mentioned only twice in the narrative, each time at a crucial point. God is mentioned in relation to Daniel's dietary protest (v. 9), and now God enters the story again: "God gave them learning and skill in all letters and wisdom; and Daniel had understanding in all visions and dreams" (Daniel 1:17).

The king imagines his training program has been successful, but there are things Nebuchadnezzar does not know and could not understand. The narrative leaves Nebuchadnezzar in his innocent self-confidence, not disabused of imperial pretensions. He does not know that Daniel violated the training program. He does not know that God, who lies beyond the reach of the king, has prevailed. He does not know that God has guarded Daniel. He does not know that God gave Daniel wisdom and a propensity for a second language. Above all, he does not know that Daniel is an utterly free man, living life on his own terms, nourished by his own faith, guarded and advanced by his own God. Nebuchadnezzar does not know. The narrative, however, is not designed for the king. Indeed, the narrative is aimed against the king, to undermine his naive self-confidence and to nullify his authority.

The conclusion of the narrative adds a nice, terse note: Daniel continued until the first year of Cyrus (v. 21).

Daniel outlasted Nebuchadnezzar. Daniel prevailed over exile, and in the process he maintained freedom in his faith. He did not conform. He did not attempt to gain or enhance his worth by conforming, nor to save his life by keeping it. Sustained by faith, Daniel is his own man as he is God's man, and he does not conform.

The text is not, I submit, remote from our own situation in which pressures in church and in society to conform are great. We imagine our worth comes in conforming, in unquestioning obedience, in responding quickly to every opinion poll of preference. The conforming happens subtly, not frontally. We join the dominant ideology with innocence and without noticing. In the congregation are those who do not notice their conformity and thus are incapable of imagining any alternative. We may notice how "the others" have conformed; we are not so skillful in noticing how we ourselves have joined the version of ideology most compatible with our social location and interest. The text invites people like us, at the door of capitulation, to think about an alternative. The proffered alternative is this: Remember *who* you are by remembering *whose* you are. Be your own person even in the face of the empire, of the dominant ideology, of the great power of death. Be your own person by being in the company of the great God who works in, with, and through the training program of the empire for the sake of God's own people. Be your own person, because God has not succumbed to the weight of the empire.

Two factors—one surprisingly hidden and one surprisingly mundane—are crucial for the working of the narrative. On the one hand, the hidden, powerful resolve of Yahweh is at work, never visible, only heard about. With cunning discernment, the narrative has recast life in the empire by noticing an extra character in the story, a character no one else had noticed. It is this awesome character whom Nebuchadnezzar will never notice, but who matters decisively. On the other hand, the story is so mundane. It matters what we eat. It matters who feeds us and on whose food we rely. Food, elemental sustenance, always comes with a price. Eat royal bread and think royal thoughts. Eat royal bread and embrace royal hopes and fears. Exiles who did not assimilate are those who know there is another bread close at hand, not provided by the Babylonians. Another poet, in some ways close to Daniel, said it this way:[10]

> Ho, every one who thirsts,
>   come to the waters;
> and he who has no money,
>   come, buy and eat!
> Why do you spend your money
>   for that which is not bread,
> and your labor for that which does not satisfy?
> Hearken diligently to me, and eat what is good,
>   and delight yourselves in fatness.[11]
> Incline your ear, and come to me;
>   hear, that your soul may live.
>
> (Isa. 55:1-3)[12]

The poet speaks of imperial bread that costs and does not satisfy. Submission to the empire causes us to labor for that which does not satisfy, that exhausts and leaves us with greater hunger.

Daniel discerned and the poet affirms, there is another bread, another wine, another milk, another nourishment, another life. It is this other food that Daniel preferred, that kept life from bondage in the empire. The great human question now is if there is another food. It is the same question troubled Jews had to ask in the time of their danger, when their Jewishness was under threat. Is there another food that will sustain? The preacher follows the poet (Isa. 55:1-3) and the narrator (Daniel 1) with an outrageous, evangelical "yes." There is another food for another life.

Later, Jesus echoes this crisis of food in the empire: "Take heed, beware of the leaven of the Pharisees and the leaven of Herod" (Mark 8:15). You know the story: the disciples "forgot the bread" (v. 14). Jesus ends that narrative with exasperation. He says, "Do you not yet understand?" (v. 21). The poet, the storyteller, and later Jesus all understand very well. Whoever feeds, owns. And we are children of another bread.

There is enough here for a biblical understanding of humanness. There is here the answer to the congregation's yearning for another way to be human in the world. The congregation gathers, close to dread conformity, sore tempted, not fully yielding, not knowing how to withstand the seduction. In the presence of the text, the issues move and grow more demanding and more ominous, more outrageous and more promissory. Now we learn that life with God has to do with exilic appetites and daring alternatives, with maintaining freedom, refusing terms, and being blessed.

The narrator of the Daniel story is a poet. He is not didactic. He neither scolds nor urges. He only proposes and imagines another way in the world.[13] The account of Daniel's great refusal is oddly impressionistic and fanciful, for in such impression and fancy come freedom. This narrative invites me to discover that my destiny with God entails a decision about conformity, empire, exile, and risk. I must decide about disciplined appetites, traveling thin, and being free. The narrative proposes new categories for reading life that tell of new possibility. Nebuchadnezzar has been duped. There is so little the empire notices. Faith, however, does not wait for the empire to catch on. Faith makes its own way in the world, all the way to the end of exile. Alternative food permits homecoming. The poet understood so well that the ones who choose different bread may go home.

The poet second Isaiah who said, "Incline your ear, and come to me; hear, that your soul may live" (Isa. 55:3) is the one who admonished exiles to seek Yahweh precisely in exile: "Seek the Lord while he may be found, call upon him while he is near" (Isa. 55:6). A few verses later, the same poet anticipates the outcome of such new eating and such faithful seeking:

> For you shall go out in joy,
>   and be led forth in peace;
> the mountains and the hills before you
>   shall break forth into singing,
>   and all the trees of the field shall
>   clap their hands.
>
> (Isa. 55:12)

Royal food takes captive. Alternative bread permits home-coming, in freedom and joy.

Daniel 1 provides one perspective on preaching the great alternative of personhood given in biblical faith. For many persons, the situation of Daniel in this narrative is not different from their own. Many persons are caught in large, unnoticing enterprises that expect conformity for the sake of success. The theme of the preacher is not nonconformity, but the freedom, energy, and courage of an alternative identity. Daniel, because he knew who he was and whose he was, was able to live outside the identity imposed on him by the empire. The gospel continues to offer such an alternative; that alternative, however, requires poetic articulation, for the alternative is as allusive and subversive as the speech in which it is uttered.

Relinquishment beyond Autonomy

The second text I consider is Daniel 4.[14] The narrative features a confrontation between Nebuchadnezzar and Daniel. Nebuchadnezzar, cipher for imperial power, embodies arrogance and high-handedness; he is, how-ever, immobilized by his dream of his own demise. Daniel is the champion of Jewish faith; he has courage and insight to interpret for the king. The story has two foci that are in some tension. One focus is the dramatic contrast between Nebuchadnezzar and Daniel, the former who ostensibly has power and loses it, the latter who ostensibly has no power but has wisdom to interpret. In terms of this dra-matic contrast, the narrative concerns the interplay of imperial power and Jewish faith.

The second focus, not fully dependent upon the first, is concerned with Nebuchadnezzar, his arrogant power, his demise, and his restoration: Nebuchadnezzar faces the inscrutable power of Yahweh who works through the power of a dream. Seen in this way, Daniel is quite incidental to the main flow of the story.

For a community under oppression as was second-century Judaism, the first focus of "Nebuchadnezzar versus Daniel" might be the more important.[15] For our purposes, I will address the second focus, namely Nebuchadnezzar in his arrogant power, who is dismantled and restored. This perspective centers on the person of Nebuchadnezzar and pays less attention to the person of Daniel. Seen in this way, the narrative becomes illuminating for our question of human personhood. Nebuchadnezzar is autonomous; or at least he thinks he is. He embodies human arrogance that imagines it is accountable to none and so is free to do whatever it wants. As a dramatic presence, he is not far removed from the ideology of autonomy of our own experience, autonomy of detached individuals who want to receive no gifts and become involved with no one, or autonomy of large concentrations of power, hierarchies, bureaucracies, nation-states that believe they live in unfettered freedom and are permitted to do whatever they can do. The premise of such autonomy is that we do not have to do with God. That of course is exactly what Nebuchadnezzar assumed. The narrative of Daniel 4 is an account of the ways in which Nebuchadnezzar was called to accountability. The main assertion of the narrative, made without direct relation to Daniel, is that the imagined autonomy of Nebuchadnezzar is not sustainable, given the reality of Yahweh.

The story of Daniel 4 begins not at the beginning, but at the end. We are given the conclusion first (vv. 1-3). In the first person singular, Nebuchadnezzar tells us the outcome of his harrowing pilgrimage from autonomy to yielding, and the painful path of his transfiguration. In his first utterance, Nebuchadnezzar speaks as a transformed man who had been drastically moved away from his autonomy. "To all peoples, nations, and languages that dwell on the earth: Peace be multiplied to you" (Dan. 4:1).[16] Nebuchadnezzar, the miliary-industrial complex in the ancient world, has been transformed into an advocate for peace. This long chapter is the tale of how that creaky complex of self-serving power was transformed by the gospel.

The recounting of transformation begins for Nebuchadnezzar in a doxology to "the Most High God," a doxology that is an act of submission, relinquishment, and yielding. Doxology is the first note in Nebuchadnezzar's transformation: his praise asserts that human life is not centered in royal autonomy but in this one who will have our devotion and obedience. The great king sings, referring to "the most High":

> How great are God's signs,
> how mighty God's wonders!
> God's kingdom is an everlasting kingdom,
> and God's dominion is from generation to generation.
> (Dan. 4:3)

The song at the beginning of Nebuchadnezzar's tale concerns God's dominion. That dominion overrides all the king's pseudo-dominion and relativizes and delegates all his pretenses. This king now has a discernment and a vision of God's true governance of the world. This initial song that establishes the context for the rule of Nebuchadnezzar is matched (vv. 34-35), at the end of the narrative, with a concluding doxology. Again Nebuchadnezzar sings to the "Most High":

> for God's dominion is an everlasting dominion,
>   and God's kingdom endures from generation
>   to generation;
> all the inhabitants of the earth are accounted as nothing;
>   and God does according to God's will
>   in the host of heaven,
>   and among the inhabitants of the earth;
> and none can stay God's hand
>   or say to God, "What doest thou?"
> (Dan. 4:34-35)

What an artistic enactment in verses 3 and 34-35, to have the long chapter framed by doxology, which is a stunning, subversive, political act![17] Our life, according to this narrative, is bracketed at the beginning and at the end by doxology. Our life is framed in praise, which is a polemical yielding, which delegitimates all other pseudo-authorities, all idolatrous claims. Human life is discerned and lived differently when our days are framed, beginning and end, with doxological statements about the true governance, against every idolatry and every ideology.[18]

Inside this doxological frame, Nebuchadnezzar recounts the route by which he yielded his power to the "Most High." The king reports, "I had a dream, and it made me afraid" (v. 5). Of course the dream frightened the king. Great, powerful people do not dream, do not intend to have nightmares, do not lose control, are not intruded upon after hours. Nebuchadnezzar and all his ilk are strong, alert, in control all day, planning, issuing memos, administering, managing, having their way. This is the way of power and privilege. Dreams bespeak vulnerability; Nebuchadnezzar imagines and pretends that he can fend off such exposure by his power and control.

There comes inevitably, however, the night, and with it weariness and sleep. With sleep there comes vulnerability and loss of control; his memos do not command and his plans do not prevail. During the day the great king manages to silence all voices but his own. He lives at ease with his autonomy and his monopoly of speech. No one is permitted to speak but the king. In the night, by contrast, the king is vulnerable, even defenseless. Voices other than his own get a chance to speak. It turns out, in such times of vulnerability, that the world is not ordered as well or as regally as he had imagined. The other voices, of God, of spirit, of the night, of darkness, penetrate the empire's Strategic Defense Initiatives. Things become unsettled, unstable, open to risk. His characteristic modes of power are less assuring. His imperial modes of knowledge are less convincing. In the nightmares of the night, even the

great king is put at risk. Nebuchadnezzar is indeed
alarmed. He is alarmed at the intrusion of God's speech
into his world, which he thought was settled and stable.

The great man, eager to contain the alarm, to cut
losses and confine the danger, summons his intelligence
community (vv. 6-7). All the dream interpreters, the people with the information, the CIA, the great ones who
manage royal knowledge, are convened. They are not able
to manage the threat of the night, however. Their modes
of power, propaganda, and ideology, their epistemology
and rationality, fail and are defeated in the face of this
powerful threat of another reality. Nebuchadnezzar discovered that his magisterial constructs of self-justification
and self-securing are indeed houses of cards. Midst his
advisors who turn out to be dysfunctional, the king begins
to sense the undoing of his imperial pretensions.

Now desperate, the king must reach outside his
government, his managed, docile world, to see if there is
some outsider who can tame the threat that is now
unleashed. "At last," says the text (v. 8), at last when all
else had failed, Nebuchadnezzar summons Daniel, the
Israelite. We are not told how Daniel is identified, known,
or summoned. He is simply there, waiting at the edge of
the story, waiting for his time of entrance when the autonomous king will notice that he is not self-sufficient.

In this poignant moment of stunning transition, the
great king comes, hat in hand, to this nobody of a Daniel.
This Daniel, whom Israel takes to be an embodiment of its
own tough, uncompromising faith, knows what the empire
does not know.[19] In his alarm and dismay, moreover, Nebuchadnezzar acknowledges this inversion of power. The
great ones have failed and this little nobody now has
authority. "I know," says Nebuchadnezzar to Daniel, "that
the spirit of the holy gods is in you and that no mystery is
too difficult for you" (Dan. 4:9). It is a remarkable conces-
sion for the great king to speak to an exile in this way. Not
only is the king no longer self-sufficient, but he must seek
help from a source inappropriate to his imagined greatness.

The narrative presents to us an epistemological crisis in which the ones who thought they knew turn out to be ignorant concerning the issues of power, authority, and certitude; conversely, the uncredentialled outsider is the one who has the knowledge that matters and can save.[20] The narrative, for hearers who are established, secured, and tenured, poses an epistemological crisis, for conventional modes of certitude and control are assaulted and dismantled.[21] It is probable that the narrative originally was intended "the other way," as a support for those without certitude, control, and official knowledge. Our own situation of reading requires that we hear the narrative, not simply as affirmation of the uncredentialled, but as dismantling of the credentialed. The narrative traces the abrupt way in which Nebuchadnezzar was moved out of his certitude into suffering, and eventually permitted hope. The narrative moves from conventional certitudes to poetic hunches.

It is indeed a remarkable dream dreamed by the king of Babylon. The dream is about the great tree in the middle of the earth (vv. 10-12). The tree was great and luxurious. All could see it. All could rely on it for orientation. The tree gave abundant fruit on which all could live. The tree gave luxuriant shade under which all could be safe. The tree ordered the world in powerful, reassuring ways.

Symbolists and interpreters have paid much attention to the character and identity of this tree.[22] Perhaps the tree could be a phallic symbol or the old tree from the Garden of Eden. Perhaps the tree, in our repeated rereading, comes to be ego strength, or Catholic orthodoxy, or *Pax Romana,* or *Pax Americana.* The tree is undoubtedly an assertion of order, strength, certainty, assurance, and reliability. The tree is free standing and self-sufficient. The tree gives to all who see it a sense that the world is coherent; it is, however, a coherence seemingly generated by the tree itself, not derived from elsewhere.

The pastoral image of the tree is interrupted by the voice of a holy one: "Cut down the tree, strip it off, scatter

the fruit, leave only a stump" (vv. 14-15). Within the world
of the dream, the voice introduces an incongruous shift of
images. The one who was the great tree becomes a beast
and must live in a jungle and eat grass (vv. 15b-16). The
words of the holy one conclude the dream with this verdict:

> . . . that the living may know that the Most High rules
> the kingdom of humankind and gives it to whom God
> will, and sets over it the lowliest of people.
>
> (Dan. 4:17)

This is a terrible dream for Nebuchadnezzar, a
dream that violates the reality and rationality by which the
empire is held together. Everything is threatened and
called into question. The narrative rendering of the dream
acknowledges there are powerful, undeniable realities
authorized by God that move against and sometimes over-
run our pretended worlds of daylight management, knowledge, and certitude. Such a nightmare as the king had robs
Nebuchadnezzar of his treasured ideology, his sense of
self-importance, his sense of self-sufficiency, and lack of
accountability. The world shaped by his claims to power
and autonomy has now been placed in deep jeopardy.

As the interpreter of the dream, Daniel is a witness
to the reality of God who overrules and subverts the king's
management of life (vv. 19-27). The narrative dares to assert
that the faith of Daniel understands the dreams that the
world dreams. The world, that is Nebuchadnezzar, wants
to stay in control and to banish such unsettling dreams.
Nebuchadnezzar wants to be protected from the vulnerability and threat of the night. Against such a self-serving
desire, however, the narrative is relentless. Dreams that
unsettle cannot be stopped, prevented, or voided. Moreover, such dreams cannot be deciphered according to the
wisdom of this age. The dream, as Nebuchadnezzar reluc-
tantly learns, requires an interpretation informed by the
reality of God's rule, an interpretation given outside royal
power and credential, an interpretation attuned to the dangerous, indomitable reality of God.

In the hands of Daniel, the dream has suddenly become an arena for prophetic indictment that is concrete and specific. Daniel says of the tree hewn down, "It is you" (v. 22).[23] Daniel does not linger to speculate over the cosmic tree and its possible mythic meaning. Daniel has moved quickly from the dream authorized by God to the concrete realities of human life that are Judaism's recurring agenda. The dream is not about a heavenly fantasy, but concerns the reality of royal power and political control in the world. This intrusive dream is a relentless voice that delegitimates human power, whether that power is expressed as political ideology, doctrinal absolutism, moralistic arrogance, or any other form of fake certitude. The dream calls to account all our careless, self-serving ideologies. The great king—the powers of this age—must learn, says Daniel, that power is in jeopardy "till you learn that the Most High rules the kingdom of humanity and gives it to whom God wills" (v. 25).

Daniel's interpretation then pushes beyond the dream in a daring act of admonition (v. 27). The dream stopped well short of urging any action upon the king. Daniel, however, dares to go beyond the data of the dream on the basis of his interpretive ethical tradition:

> Therefore, O king, let my counsel be acceptable to you; break off your sins by practicing righteousness, and your iniquities by showing mercy to the oppressed, that there may perhaps be a lengthening of your tranquility.
>
> (Dan. 4:27)

Daniel urges Nebuchadnezzar to accept a radically different characterization of power and of reality. Dominion is translated into righteousness and the practice of caring fidelity (cf. Mark 10:42-44). Control is transformed into mercy for the oppressed, all those on whose backs the empire was built. This imperative in the mouth of Daniel requires a complete renovation of the empire. Daniel's imperative envisions "bringing to nought the things that are" (1 Cor. 1:28), the emergence of something genuinely new, "calling into existence things that do not exist" (Rom. 4:17).

The outcome of such a radical renovation, says Daniel, may be "tranquility" (*selevah*). Daniel dares to say to the king, the tranquility you desire and pursue will not come by greater control. Tranquility is not given in the categories of royal self-sufficiency. There is not enough royal knowledge or royal power to stop the subverting dream from surging in the night. There is not enough royal ideology to flatten the dream into an imperial program. There may perhaps be length of days for tranquility, but those days are granted only with the most elemental and determined commitment to righteousness and mercy. The well-being the king craves can come in no other way.

Such a recasting of the dream into ethical demand does not happen because Daniel is the voice of crazy radicalism. The demand is given because Daniel has understood that no amount of strident control or imagined autonomy can finally nullify the simple God-ordained requirement of mercy and compassion. The bedrock of mercy and righteousness is not negotiable. The dreams besetting the royal world in its anguished nights of troubled sleep are not escapist fantasies, but are a summons to get right with the neighbor. Such getting right is costly and unsettling. Daniel's faith is an insistence that the vision of the night be rendered into urgency of daytime policy and practice. The world will have neither tranquility nor well-being, until the horrors of the night are transformed to newness in the day.

Predictably, the anticipation of the nightmare came to reality. What Nebuchadnezzar dreamed (vv. 10-18), what Daniel interpreted (vv. 19-27), is set in motion (vv. 28-33). Like most of us most of the time, Nebuchadnezzar found his alarming dream too demanding, so he ignored it. He thought it would pass. The dream required Nebuchadnezzar to quit being who he had been. In his obduracy and his self-regard, he changes nothing about his life or his power. He arrives at the office the next day as though he had not dreamed, as though he had rested peaceably, when in fact he had tossed and turned all night with a vision of his own undoing. When his executive secretary inquired about his night he answered, "Oh, I slept well, thank you."

A year later, Nebuchadnezzar is still self-assured (vv. 28-30). In the daytime there was no concrete threat to correspond to the odd, dismissed voice of the night. Perhaps he had only "imagined" the dream. The king walked on the roof of his royal palace, undiminished, unworried, imagining that the dream had been nullified, and that he would, in his autonomous world, go on and on. He said in his arrogance: "Is not this great Babylon, which I have built by my mighty power as a royal residence and for the glory of my majesty?" (Dan. 4:30) His words anticipate those of the man in Jesus' parable who also said:

> What shall I do, for I have nowhere to store my crops. . . . I will do this; I will pull down my barns, and build larger ones; and there I will store all my grain and my goods. And I will say to my soul, Soul, you have ample goods laid up for many years; take your ease, eat, drink, be merry.
>
> (Luke 12:17-19)

The king's voice of self-congratulations seems normal, given the world's odd notion of conversation. The world prefers speech reduced to monologue, in which we hear only our own voice, as though the conversation always includes only one, unchallenged voice.

The narrative about Nebuchadnezzar (as in Jesus' parable) is ruthless and uncompromising. "While the words were still in the king's mouth . . . " (v. 31). Nebuchadnezzar had not even finished his wonderful, propagandistic self-deception, when there came another voice, a voice from outside the empire that the king could not silence. This other voice turns out to be the decisive voice in the entire drama. When that voice speaks, Nebuchadnezzar is reduced to silence. The king dare utter no answer. The intruding voice of the gospel takes initiative away from

Nebuchadnezzar (and from us). This is an odd, inexplicable voice; it is, however, welcomed by the narrator and treated as though it is a proper counter to the voice of the king. This other voice, said to be a voice "from heaven," says:

> O King Nebuchadnezzar, to you it is spoken: The kingdom has departed from you, and you shall be driven from among humanity.
>
> (Dan. 4:31-32a)
>
> The tree becomes a beast " . . . until you learn that the Most High rules the kingdom of humanity and gives it to whom God will."
>
> (Dan. 4:32)

Immediately, the speech from heaven came to fruition (v. 33)! We watch while the great king is dismantled. The dismantling in this text is more immediate and more abrupt than most of our experienced dismantling. Most of our experience is slower and moves only gradually. We watch while our seasons of arrogance and autonomy slowly come to a sorry end. We watch now while colonialism around the world slowly expires. We watch while brutality eventually turns on its perpetrators. We watch closer to home while our small, gradual tyrannies collapse, our little self-deceptions cave in, and our modern intimidations fail. We find ourselves, little by little, destabilized, cut off from our intended modes of control.

Our experienced slowness and this narrative immediacy, however, come to the same thing—trees cut down, kings become beasts, worlds subverted, security shattered, power undone, illusions exposed. We are embarrassed to discover in our experience, as in the narrative, that we are not at all whom we imagined and announced ourselves to be. The royal monologue is intruded upon by a more compelling voice that is enacted "immediately."

The narrative, however, is not simply a flat dismissal of royal arrogance. There is a counter theme that can only come at the end of the story (vv. 34-37). Nebuchadnezzar has indeed been reduced to a humiliated silence. But in

v. 34, he has recovered his voice. He speaks again. His voice now for the first time takes into account the overriding reality of God. Nebuchadnezzar has abandoned his pretense and self-deception and for the first time sees his life in true perspective, shorn of autonomy.

He says, "I lifted up my eyes to heaven" (v. 34). I looked beyond myself. I acknowledged a rule other than my own. When the king looks beyond himself, he is also able to say, "My reason (*manda'*) returned." His capacity to discern had been lost in his arrogant drive for autonomy and control. Becoming autonomous had caused Nebuchadnezzar to lose his reason (that is, to go crazy). When he yielded his eyes to heaven and his life to God, his sense came back.[24] Reason, as Nebuchadnezzar learned, is faith seeking understanding through obedience.[25] Astonishingly, he is rehabilitated. He is reclothed in a rightful mind (cf. Mark 5:15). He is given back his throne and his power.

The gospel is not simply a story of destabilization, subversion, and abasement. It is also a story of gifts given, new grants of power and authority, freedom to govern, and joy in well-being. This is, however, a new grant received in yielding, a fresh authorization grounded in a terrible relinquishment, a fresh joy triggered by a dismantling nightmare, a new birth of power out of a death of old self-deception.[26]

Nebuchadnezzar now tells us, at the end of the tale, why he began his account with doxology in verse 3. It is because new life, new power, new authority begin in doxology. The song at the end of the dream narrative becomes the warrant for a new beginning of royal authority and governance. The world, and its powerful human actors, may expect to be born again ("from above"), to have new life, to have power reauthorized and dominion reconstituted.[27] The restoration of Nebuchadnezzar, however, is on new terms, terms other than had been assumed by the king. The restoration and reconstitution are on the terms given by the "Most High," the one with whom Nebuchadnezzar finally must deal.

This Nebuchadnezzar-Daniel narrative provides rich substance for preaching. Listening to the sermon are many who have succumbed to the world of Nebuchadnezzar, imagining they are free, on their own, unencumbered, not needing to respond or answer. Nebuchadnezzar has reduced his life so that everything he touched was under his control. Or so he thought.

The dream, however, pushes against this self-deception. The dream is an act of subversion and therefore acute discomfort. The dream is also a modest, tortured yearning for an alternative. The dream is both threat and hope: threat about the loss of this house of cards that cannot stand, hope to be in a serious conversation with one who can order and govern the wild reality only seemingly under control. The dream is an odd event in which God is subject and the king is receptive object. We, the preacher and the congregation, are invited to watch while we see this presumedly autonomous person brought forcibly back into a relation of mutuality where he can live differently. While we watch Nebuchadnezzar's wrenching transformation, we are invited to our own.

The substance of this narrative will preach. But the form of the narrative is equally important. In this narrative, we have modeled for us a way in which to communicate to the autonomous, imperial sovereigns in our midst. Those like Nebuchadnezzar, insulated in their self-deception and surrounded by "yes-men" and "yes-women," cannot be addressed frontally. Daniel could not have stormed into the royal cabinet meeting with a denunciation. Such an approach would have been on the turf and on the terms of the emperor, and Daniel would have been silenced and eliminated. In like manner, the preacher can scarcely conduct a frontal assault against victims of autonomy, for the preacher will then be silenced and perhaps eliminated. In this narrative, the manner of the gospel is not frontal assault, but the slow, hidden impression of dream that comes like a thief in the night to rob the king of his mistaken identity. It is that fanciful communication, made when the royal muscles are relaxed and the king is vulnerable, that creates a fresh moment of discernment. Whereas confrontation may only reinforce the autonomy, this artistic move outside the control of the king has a chance. I am speaking, of course, of poetic discourse that takes the king by surprise, that makes him wonder beyond his certitude, that makes him ask beyond his answers, that makes him seek beyond his rationality. It is the poet who comes in the darkness, which the king does not administer. In spite of a defended reduction, the king heeds the voice of the dream. The king does not fully censure the dark invasion of trouble from on high.

In spite of everything being settled, the king is transformed to terms other than his own. Like Daniel in the first chapter who is shaped by an identity the empire could not give or take away, so in this chapter even the king is enabled to accept an identity other than the one given in the empire. In the end, even the autonomous king is freed for a new life, as freed as Daniel who refused conformity. Taken together, Daniel in courage and Nebuchadnezzar in dread receive liberated identities. It is the same liberated identity that may be offered and mediated on the lips of the preacher who speaks underneath our destructive reductions.

The Word Will Do

The preacher speaks among people who yearn to have their lives shaped and characterized by the intrusion of God. That yearning, however, has become so conventional and so familiar among us that it is reduced, distorted, and misunderstood. The yearning for a connection to God, on the one hand, leads to *docility* before a God too sovereign, and derivatively, docility before every visible power. On the other hand, the same yearning leads to *autonomy* before a God too accommodating, and derivatively autonomy in the face of every social requirement.[28]

In such a situation of docility and autonomy, the preacher must sound the gospel. The claim of the gospel is already well- and long-known, even by those who have reduced the gospel to docility or to autonomy. The preacher has entrusted to her a claim too-long believed, too-innocently yearned for, so believed and yearned for that it is largely empty of power and rendered innocuous. Because of the reductions that render the gospel empty and innocuous, the preacher must speak against the reductions to permit a fresh hearing. The fresh hearing must be in new, artistic forms, so that the speaking and the hearing are done with fresh imagination, with new power, and with authorizing energy that takes us by surprise.

These two narratives in Daniel 1 and Daniel 4 model what must be artistically offered by the preacher concerning the character of human life. In Daniel 1, Daniel is in a situation where conformity and docility seemed to serve best as a clue to successful behavior. Daniel's immediate temptation was conformity to imperial power. Daniel might have perceived the imperial enterprise as absolute, and so requiring absolute obedience. It is precisely Daniel's linkage to the God of Israel that precludes such conformity. Daniel's relation to his God is one of mutuality, for it is Daniel's resolve in verse 8 that precedes and evokes God's favor and compassion in verse 9. It is Daniel's capacity to act in freedom that changes his relation both to the empire and to the God who will bless him.

Against Daniel's temptation to docility and conformity, the narrative explicates another, "more excellent way" to be in the empire. Daniel's "more excellent way" in the world is to resist docility, to practice an alternative way in the world that requires courage, involves risk, and ends in freedom. Daniel is a person (and a model) who embraces faithfulness as a daring alternative to docility. By the end of the narrative, Daniel's bold resistance is celebrated. He has maintained his freedom before the king.

Conversely, in Daniel 4, Nebuchadnezzar is in a situation where autonomy and self-sufficiency seem to be an appropriate way in the world. Because of his enormous power, Nebuchadnezzar thought himself accountable to none. Were he a religious man, he would imagine that God had given all things into his hand.[29] Nebuchadnezzar does not, however, bother to reflect on the source of what he has been given. He only knows he has power; he imagines that he has always had it, and that he will always have it as his absolute possession. Against such a temptation to autonomy, the narrative explicates another "more excellent way." Nebuchadnezzar's "more excellent way" in the world is to abandon his autonomy, to practice another way that receives the terrible dream, responds to the demand of covenant, and finally yields to the Most High in doxology.

Both Daniel and Nebuchadnezzar act for an alternative way in the world, resolute Daniel by *daring resistance,* chastened Nebuchadnezzar by *yielding doxology.* Daniel comes out of a situation of political oppression by his great refusal. Nebuchadnezzar comes out of a situation of self-destructive arrogance by his desperate yielding. In the end Daniel is celebrated in the world where he seemed to have no chance, for he is "ten times better" (1:20). In the end, Nebuchadnezzar is acknowledged as powerful before the throne of God, where he did not want to go: "still more greatness was added to me" (Dan. 4:36). Daniel seemed to have no chance before Nebuchadnezzar, but he has gained the capacity to be his own man. Nebuchadnezzar seemed to have no chance before Yahweh, but he has found sanity and peace, as well as power, in yielding.

In conclusion, I note one other matter that is important for appropriating these narratives. Nebuchadnezzar and Daniel are oddly present in each other's story. Daniel 1 is all about Daniel; Daniel, however, must find his way around in the presence of Nebuchadnezzar's awesome power. Daniel 4 is all about Nebuchadnezzar; Nebuchadnezzar, however, finds his way only because he receives clues from the newly emancipated Daniel. Nebuchadnezzar and Daniel have finally to do with each other. Neither

story will work for the central character without the other
as the "best supporting actor." The two stories and their
two main characters cannot be separated from each other.

God's new humanity requires *the courage of great
resistance:* resistance to every enslavement, refusal of every
cooptation in heaven or on earth, a resolve to be one's
own person. God's new humanity requires at the same
time the *bold practice of doxology:* engagement with the
dream in all its threat, submission, and relinquishment in
order to be safe. How odd, how inescapably true, that our
yearning for God requires both *the resistance of Daniel* and
the relinquishment of Nebuchadnezzar—the enactment of daring freedom and the embrace of awesome doxology. The
two characters and their two responses must go together,
because we are always both Daniel and Nebuchadnezzar:
like Daniel tempted to submit and called to resist, like
Nebuchadnezzar, tempted to autonomy and called to
relinquish.

The two narratives of Daniel 1 and Daniel 4, like our
world, begin with the issue of royal command and imperial decree. The biblical narrative, however, forms a coun-
terproposal. It tells a story designed to break the system.
The narrative violates the command and shatters the
decree. The artistic rendering of the narrative offers an
alternative to the frozenness of royal assertion that eventually would destroy both Nebuchadnezzar and Daniel.
The narrative eludes imperial rationality and is another
instance in which "finally comes the poet." The poet is
always voicing an alternative that is subverting and inviting, nullifying and authorizing.

It is only artistic narrative that can tell of the daring
option of Daniel as he moves from the chief of the eunuchs
to the steward, to ten days of testing, until he is finally
"ten times better." It is only artistic narrative that can tell
of the journey of dread for Nebuchadnezzar as he moves
from the threat of the dream, to its interpretation, enactment, and resolve. Both narrative accounts track, step by
step, the end of an old world, of docility and of autonomy.

The narrative lets us watch while Daniel resists in order to have freedom, and while Nebuchadnezzar relinquishes for sanity. It may be as important as it is odd that our textual base for an alternative humanity is found in these peculiar tales, scarcely reasonable, telling more than is explained, voicing what the regime preferred to silence. It takes such poetic rendering to move beyond the seduction of command (Daniel 1) and the seduction of decree (Daniel 4) to another life in the empire.

Conclusion

The Daniel narratives provide an appropriate ending point for my larger argument, for they voice in particular the theme I have addressed in each of these chapters. In each case I have suggested that prose-reductionism of the gospel has led our believing society to misappropriate the promise of the gospel. The misappropriation has led to the distortion of life (as of faith) that variously ends in numbness and ache, alienation and rage, restlessness and greed, conformity and autonomy. It is odd and agonizing that a public community so attentive to the claims of this tradition can so widely misunderstand and embrace in distorted ways the gifts that are offered.

It is in this context that the preacher must dare to speak what is already believed but so little understood, so little embraced, so little trusted, so little practiced. We are agreed together that the hope of the gospel is indeed healing, communion, obedience, and freedom. Those good gifts, however, are often unavailable in the bosom of our common belief.

It is this situation of incongruity in which the preacher must voice an alternative much yearned for and deeply feared. In that situation of fearful, yet hopeful, reductionism, the preacher speaks in another language, a language not frontal but subtle, a voice not assaulting but surprising, speech not predictable but faithful in its daring. That other language of evangelical possibility is spoken with the gentle quiet of a dove, with the dread-filled cunning of a serpent.

Despite the seeming odds against the poem, however, despite the awesome challenge of the task, perhaps better, *because of* the odds and the challenge, the preacher must speak. Our lives wait in the balance, hoping, yearning for the promissory, transforming word of the gospel. In the end, all we have is the word of the gospel. There are evidences and signs all around us, however, in the great brutal confrontations of public power and in the weeping hiddenness of hurt in persons, that this odd speech of the gospel matters decisively. We have only the word, but the word will do.[30] It will do because it is true that the poem shakes the empire, that the poem heals and transforms and rescues, that the poem enters like a thief in the night and gives new life, fresh from the word and from nowhere else.

There are many pressures to quiet the text, to silence this deposit of dangerous speech, to halt this outrageous practice of speaking alternative possibility. The poems, however, refuse such silence. They will sound. They sound through preachers who risk beyond prose. In the act of such risk, power is released, newness is evoked, God is praised. People are "speeched" to begin again. Such new possibility is offered in daring speech. Each time that happens, "finally comes the poet"—finally.

Notes

INTRODUCTION

1. This premise is parallel to and informed by the argument of Fred Craddock, *Overhearing the Gospel* (Nashville: Abingdon Press, 1978).

2. On the problem of skepticism as a view of the world that precludes mystery, see Daniel W. Hardy and David F. Ford, *Praising and Knowing God* (Philadelphia: Westminster Press, 1985), 108–22.

3. On the power of ideology to distort the gospel, see Walter Brueggemann, *Israel's Praise: Doxology against Idolatry and Ideology* (Philadelphia: Fortress Press, 1988), esp. chap. 4.

4. Andrew Greeley, *The New York Times Book Review* (XCI 12, 1986), 3, has nicely articulated the reality of such distortion: "The only real Jesus is one who is larger than life, who escapes our categories, who eludes our attempts to reduce Him for our cause. Any Jesus who has been made to fit our formula ceases to be appealing precisely because He is no longer wondrous, mysterious, surprising. We may reduce Him to a right-wing Republican conservative or a gun-toting Marxist revolutionary and thus rationalize and justify our own political ideology. But having done so, we are dismayed to discover that whoever we have signed on as an ally is not Jesus. Categorize Jesus and He isn't Jesus anymore."

5. Robert Lifton, *Living and Dying* (New York: Praeger, 1974), 137, has written of a "symbol gap" when there are no religious symbols that are adequate to mediate experience. In

such a gap, we become numb, and when numb, are capable of brutality. Positivistic, technical reason urges and embodies the banishment of liberated, liberating symbols.

6. On such destructive modes of communication, see Jacques Ellul, *Propaganda: The Formulation of Men's Attitudes* (New York: Knopf, 1965); idem, *The Humiliation of the Word* (Grand Rapids: Eerdmans Publishing Co., 1985); and Wendell Berry, *Standing by Words* (San Francisco: North Point Press, 1983), esp. 24–63.

7. Concerning an open universe of discourse and its reduction and closure, see Herbert Marcuse, *One Dimensional Man* (Boston: Beacon Press, 1964), esp. chap. 4. Carol Gilligan (*In a Different Voice* [Cambridge, Mass.: Harvard University Press, 1982]), has made an important argument for more than one voice in the social conversation. If I understand rightly, the argument of George A. Lindbeck (*The Nature of Doctrine* [Philadelphia: Westminster Press, 1984]) is to insist on the distinctive language of the church as the voice in which the church must speak, if it is to be faithful.

8. Jurgen Habermas, *Legitimation Crisis* (Boston: Beacon Press, 1974), 105, 121, has seen most clearly how the practice of communication can either form or preclude serious community. His "ideal speech situation" is an important model for the church to consider in its own life.

9. See Walter Brueggemann, "The Third World of Evangelical Imagination," *Horizons in Biblical Theology,* 8.2 (1986): 61–84.

10. George Anastapo, *The Artist As Thinker* (Chicago: Swallow Press, 1983), 11. Amos Wilder, *Theopoetic* (Philadelphia: Fortress Press, 1976), has explicated the poetic dimension of religious imagination.

11. Hans Urs von Balthasar, "The Glory of the Lord," *A Theological Aesthetics* I (New York: Crossroad, 1982),: 43, in part quoted F. Medicus.

12. Wallace Stevens, "Notes Toward a Supreme Fiction," see Mary Gerhart and Allen Russell, *Metaphoric Process: The Creation of Scientific and Religious Understanding* (Fort Worth, Tex.: Texas Christian University Press, 1984), 161, and David Daiches, *God and the Poets* (Oxford: Oxford University Press, 1983), 72.

13. Garrett Green, " 'The Bible As . . . ': Fictional Narrative and Scriptural Truth,"in *Scriptural Authority and Narrative Interpretation,* ed. Garrett Green (Philadelphia: Fortress Press, 1987), 94.

14. Walt Whitman, "Passage to India," 5:101–5 *Leaves of Grass* (New York: Mentor Books, The New American Library, 1954), 324.

15. Robert Alter, *The Art of Biblical Narrative* (New York: Basic Books, 1981), has written about the power of biblical narrative. More generally the same affirmations are valid concerning the elusive, poetic speech of the biblical tradition: "But in the First commonwealth period, there seems to have been an unequaled happy conjunction of available possibilities of narrative expression with the new sense of man, God and history that was just taking root in some vital sectors of national consciousness. The monotheistic revolution was, I think, a necessary condition but by no means sufficient one for the revolution in narrative art . . . There is an essential residue of the unexplainable in artistic creation."

16. Anastapto, *Artist Thinker*, 11, concludes: "Thus the right kind of art—that is, again, genuine art—discovers the sense of the universe and man's place in it, if only by reminding us of and refining the enduring questions, including questions both about what it means to know and what is truly knowable."

17. It is this foundational decision about the authority of the text as a theological voice that is the counterpart to canon. "Canon Criticism," as in the work of Brevard S. Childs, proceeds on the basis of such a religious decision and conviction.

18. Edward Farley, *Theologia* (Philadelphia: Fortress Press, 1983), has argued that the traditional, "house of authority" has collapsed, the probing community does not concede this judgment. Letty Russell, *Household of Freedom* (Philadelphia: Westminster Press, 1987), chap. 4 and esp. p. 64, responds to Farley, suggesting the "house of authority" has been under the wrong management, i.e., partriarchal, authoritarian management.

19. Amos Wilder, *Jesus' Parables and the War of Myths: Essays on Imagination in the Scriptures* (Philadelphia: Fortress Press, 1982), has understood that various stories and story-worlds are in deep conflict and compete with each other for our adherence.

20. The theme is well pursued by Gail R. O'Day, *The Word Disclosed* (St. Louis: CBP Press, 1987). O'Day shrewdly sees how the way of speech is correlated with the way of the new world. The new world comes in the new rendering of the words.

21. On the theme of imagination assaulting ideology, see the same argument of Stanley Hauerwas, "From System to

Story: An Alternative Pattern for Rationality in Ethics," *Truthfulness and Tragedy* (Notre Dame, Ind.: University of Notre Dame Press, 1977), 15–30. The assault of story on system is a variation on the same transaction. The claim of the literature and the practice of storytelling is based in the conviction that the story can indeed penetrate the system.

1: NUMBNESS AND ACHE

1. On the metaphor of weaving, see Peter M. Morgan, *Story Weaving: Using Stories to Transform Your Congregation* (St. Louis: CBP Press, 1986).

2. The three moves of which I am speaking are the central themes of evangelical faith. The themes are expressed in another way in the second question and answer in the *Heidelberg Catechism:* "How many things must you know that you may live and die in the blessedness of this comfort?" "Three. First, the greatness of my sin and wretchedness. Second, How I am freed from all sins and their wretched consequences. Third, what gratitude I owe to God for such redemption."

3. For a recent discussion of "deadly sins," see Donald Capps, *Deadly Sins and Saving Virtues* (Philadelphia: Fortress Press, 1987).

4. On embarrassment as a religious practice, see Abraham Heschel, *Who Is Man?* (Stanford: Stanford University Press, 1965), 112–14. Robert J. Lifton, *The Broken Connection* (New York: Simon and Schuster, 1980), has discerned the potentially positive function of real guilt in relation to ethical questions. Lifton has explored in many places the deathly outcome of numbness that no longer notices or acknowledges.

5. On "rendering" God, see Dale Patrick, *The Rendering of God in the Old Testament* (Philadelphia: Fortress Press, 1981).

6. In the two places where we might expect an accent on guilt, it is not articulated. On the one hand, the cultic perception of reality in the book of Leviticus is not preoccupied with guilt but with the concrete ways in which God makes forgiveness and reconciliation possible. Leviticus is about "the means of grace." On the other hand, the psalms, and especially the psalms of lament, comment on the "human predicament." In these poems, however, even in the "Pauline Psalms," there is no great preoccupation with guilt, but with address to the God who can extricate Israel from the predicament. In both these literatures, the backdrop of guilt is cited only as a beginning point. The real focus is on the God who can transform such situations.

7. On this engagement of God with God's people, Hyam Macoby, "Overruling the Voice from Heaven," *New York Times Book Review* (Nov. 10, 1985), 24, in a review of *A Living Covenant* by David Hartman has written, " . . . so the humanism of Judaism is accompanied by continual awareness of the presence and approval of God—who is like a parent rejoicing when his child displays independence and initiative." Such a God cannot be reduced to a mechanical principle of retribution.

8. Don Browning, *The Moral Context of Pastoral Care* (Philadelphia: Westminster Press, 1976), has forcefully articulated the moral dimension of pastoral care. That moral dimension must be heeded in liturgy in which the community of faith is met by the one on the throne.

9. See the poignant discussion of this text by Kazo Kitamora, *Theology of the Pain of God* (Richmond: John Knox Press, 1965).

10. Understanding cult as an act of God's grace is surely the intent of the texts themselves. They were not seen or intended to be seen as magical, manipulative, or mechanical, but as a means of grace given by God. This is in opposition to the usual view (especially held among Protestants) that cult is only a device of human manipulation. See Brevard S. Childs, *Old Testimony Theology in a Canonical Context* (Philadelphia: Fortress Press, 1985), 155–74.

11. See the stunning analysis of the history of this conflict in Walter LaFeber, *Inevitable Revolutions* (New York: Norton Press, 1983), and Roy Gutman, *Banana Diplomacy: The Making of American Policy in Nicaragua* (New York: Simon and Schuster, 1988).

12. On the theme of justice, see Brueggemann, "Voices of the Night—Against Justice," *To Act Justly, Love Tenderly, Walk Humbly,* (New York: Paulist Press, 1986), 5.

13. On the economic dimension of this petition, see Michael Crosby, *Thy Will Be Done: Praying the Our Father as Subversive Activity* (Maryknoll, N.Y.: Orbis, 1977), chap. 8, and Sharon Ringe, *Jesus, Liberation, and the Jubilee Year* (Philadelphia: Fortress Press, 1985).

14. My use of the phrase has been powerfully reinforced by J. Glenn Gray, *The Warriors* (New York: Harper and Row, 1959), chap. 6, which is entitled, "The Ache of Guilt."

15. Iris Murdoch, *The Red and the Green* (New York: The Viking Press, 1965), 188–92.

16. On the odd transactions that make forgiveness possible, see the discerning comments of John Patton, "Human

Forgiveness as Problem and Discovery," *Christian Century* 102 (1985): 795.

17. See Robert A. Guelich, *The Sermon on the Mount* (Waco, Tex.: Word Books, 1982), 240–41.

18. The reference to "evil conscience" in the text of Hebrews 10 does not refer to a "guilty feeling" or to any other psychological phenomenon. It refers rather to the reality of having wronged God and being cut off from access to God. This distinction is important, lest the problem of guilt be trivialized as has happened in our conventional reductionism. On the persistent distortion in Christian interpretation, see Krister Stendahl, "The Apostle Paul and the Introspective Conscience of the West," *HTR* 56 (1963): 199–215.

19. Gustav Aulen, *Christus Victor* (New York: Macmillan, 1969), has reviewed the several "theories of atonement" that have dominated Christian theology, and has made a compelling case why the theory of God's victory in Christ is most congenial to evangelical faith. This theory he contrasts with and commends over the theories of "satisfaction" and "moral influence." My argument here is of another kind. What is needed is not only one or more theories, but poetic imagination to voice many words, figures, images, and metaphors—none of which is adequate—to state the claim of the gospel. It is clear that the richness of the Bible moved in many directions and was not contained or domesticated by any limited range of "theories."

20. On the tense and necessary juxtaposition of these hymnic, theological traditions, see Shirley G. Guthrie Jr., *Diversity in Faith, Unity in Christ* (Philadelphia: Westminster Press, 1986).

21. Julian of Norwich (*Showings* [New York: Paulist Press, 1978], 149) has said these words in classic formulation: "But all will be well, and every kind of thing will be well."

2: ALIENATION AND RAGE

1. Robert N. Bellah, et. al, *Habits of the Heart* (Berkeley and Los Angeles: University of California Press, 1985).

2. Alasdair MacIntyre, *After Virtue* (Notre Dame, Ind.: University of Notre Dame Press, 1981), 29–31, 70–75.

3. Jonathan Kozol, *Rachel and Her Children: Homeless Families in America* (New York: Crown Publishers, 1988), 34–35, has a poignant characterization of the cruciality of "Thou." He quotes a hopeless, homeless woman: "The Bible is what taught

me to read. When I read those 'thee's' and 'thou's,' I have this dream. God comes to me. He calls me 'thee.' I call him 'Thou.' "

4. Daniel Yankelovich, *New Rules: Searching for Self-Fulfillment in a World Turned Upside Down* (New York: Random House, 1981) has explored the social reaction against an ethic of rules in the form of psychology of self-actualization. That is, subjectivism is a reaction against excessive objectivism. It is possible, I suggest, to correlate this twofold distortion of real communion with the theological modes of George A. Linkbeck, *The Nature of Doctrine* (Philadelphia: Westminster Press, 1984). His "cognitive-propositional" dimension relates to what I have called objectivism, his "experiential-expressive" dimension correlates to what I have called subjective. In my analysis I am suggesting that both are forms of theological reductionism that distort the claims of biblical faith.

5. While it is not very well articulated, clearly the issue of theodicy is on the minds of many people. This is evidenced in the remarkable popularity of Harold S. Kushner's *When Bad Things Happen to Good People* (New York: Schocken Books, 1981), which is not a very convincing settlement of the theodic question. More helpfully see William H. Willimon, *Speaking for Eden* (Nashville: Abingdon Press, 1985); Terence E. Fretheim, *The Suffering of God* (Philadelphia: Fortress Press, 1984); Douglas John Hall, *God and Human Suffering* (Minneapolis: Augsburg, 1986); and J. Christian Beker, *Suffering and Hope: The Biblical Vision and the Human Predicament* (Philadelphia: Fortress Press, 1987).

6. On the potential ideological force of liturgy, see Brueggemann, *Israel's Praise: Doxology Against Idolatry and Ideology* (Philadelphia: Fortress Press, 1988), chap. 4.

7. See the discerning comments of Gordon D. Kaufman, *Theology for a Nuclear Age* (Philadelphia: Westminster Press, 1985). Kaufman indicates how conventional theology leads to abdication of human responsibility for the danger of nuclear weapons. (See especially chap. 1). See also Leonard I. Sweet, *The Lion's Pride* (Nashville: Abingdon Press, 1987) and A. G. Mojtabai, *Blessed Assurance: At Home with the Bomb in Amarillo, Texas* (New York: Houghton Mifflin, 1986).

8. Lucy Bregman (*Through the Landscape of Faith.* [Philadelphia: Westminster Press, 1986]) has explored the ways in which the dynamics of Christian sacraments counter such destructive modes of living.

9. Robert Alter, *The Art of Biblical Poetry* (New York: Basic Books, 1985), 212.

10. On the destruction of self by the loss of speech, see the alarming analysis of Elaine Scarry, *The Body in Pain* (New York: Oxford University Press, 1985). She makes clear that as torture destroys humanness, so speech creates humanness. Much of the effort of liberation theology is concerned with the recovery of speech among the silenced and muted.

11. Emil Fackenheim (*God's Presence in History* [San Francisco: Harper and Row, 1970], 14–16) has spoken of the "saving and commanding divine presence."

12. On the structure of the lament psalms, see Claus Westermann, *The Psalms: Structure, Content and Message* (Minneapolis: Augsburg, 1980), chaps. 1 and 3; Bernhard W. Anderson, *Out of the Depths* (Philadelphia: Westminster Press, 1983), 5–77; Walter Brueggemann, *The Message of the Psalms* (Minneapolis: Augsburg, 1984), 51–58, and Patrick D. Miller Jr., *Interpreting the Psalms* (Philadelphia: Fortress Press, 1986), 48–63.

13. Alter, *Biblical Poetry*, 67–73, offers a discerning analysis of the poem with particular attention to the matter of silence and speech.

14. Erhard Gerstenberger, "Der klagende Mensch," *Probleme biblischer Theologie*, ed. Hans Walter Wolff (Munich: Chr. Kaiser Verlag, 1971), 64–72, has shown that the complaint is indeed an act of hope and a refusal to accept in resignation the present circumstance.

15. On the legitimacy and cruciality of protest in an honest faith, see the remarks of Isaac Bashevis Singer and Richards Burgin, in *Conversations with Isaac Bashevis Singer* (Garden City, N.Y.: Doubleday and Co., 1985), 174–78.

16. Karl Barth, *Prayer* (Philadelphia: Westminster Press, 1952), 26, has explored this twofold aspect of prayer. On the one hand, we are commanded to pray. On the other hand, we are expected to pray with freedom and audacity.

17. See Walter Brueggemann, "Theological Education: Hearing the Blind Beggar," *The Christian Century* 103 (1986): 114–6.

18. See Walter Brueggemann, "A Shape for Old Testament Theology, II: Embrace of Pain," *CBQ* 47 (1985): 395–415.

19. It is plausible to suggest that the question posed to Yahweh by Abraham comes to resolution in the self-discernment of God in the pathos of Hos. 11:8–9. See Walter Brueggemann, *Genesis: An Interpretation* (Atlanta: John Knox Press, 1982) and J. Gerald Janzen, "Metaphor and Reality in Hosea 11," *Semeia* 24 (1982): 7–44. The allusion to Sodom and Gomorrah in Hos. 11:8–9 suggests an intentional connection

between the question posed by Abraham in Genesis 18 and the resolve of God in Hosea 11.

20. Walter Baumgartner, *Jeremiah's Poem of Lament* (Sheffield, Wis.: Sheffield Academic Press, 1988).

21. On the phrase, see Shelden Vanaulsen, *A Severe Mercy* (San Francisco: Harper and Row, 1977).

22. Gerhard von Rad (*Wisdom in Israel* [Nashville: Abingdon Press, 1972], 64–65) interprets "folly" in Israel as "practical atheism." "Folly is a lack of order in a man's most innermost being, a lack which defies all instruction; often, indeed, folly is regarded as something which cannot be corrected (e.g., Prov. 27:22). . . . This lack of realism also included a misjudging of God himself. The fool 'rages' against God (Prov. 19:3). Later, the same idea was formulated in more basic theological terms, 'The fool says in his heart, "There is no God" ' (Ps. 14:1). Folly is practical atheism." See also p. 83. It is interesting to move from von Rad's understanding of folly as atheism to the several case studies in folly offered by Barbara W. Tuchman, *The March of Folly* (New York: Ballantine Books, 1984).

23. On the whirlwind speeches of God as a genuine answer to Job, see James A. Wharton, "The Unanswerable Answer: An Interpretation of Job," *Texts and Testaments*, ed. W. Eugene March (San Antonio: Trinity University Press, 1980), 37–70. See also Donald E. Gowan, "God's Answer to Job: Is It an Answer?" *Horizons in Biblical Theology* 82 (1986): 85–102. On the dialogical character of Job, see Claus Westermann, *The Structure of the Book of Job* (Philadelphia: Fortress Press, 1981). Gustavo Gutierrez, *On Job* (Maryknoll, N.Y.: Orbis Books, 1987), has recently explored the ways in which the poem of Job is an exploration of new forms of speech appropriate to the restlessness of the suffering. Gutierrez has introduced a much-needed element of social criticism into our reading of Job.

24. On the destabilizing, inviting intention of the speeches from the whirlwind, see Walter Brueggemann, "The Third World of Evangelical Imagination," *Horizons in Biblical Theology* 82 (1986): 61–84.

25. The answering speech of Yahweh characteristically asserts Yahweh's attentiveness to and solidarity with the one complaining. It characteristically includes a promise that there will be a transformative intervention. The circumstantial evidence for this caring, transformative answer is that the prayer regularly turns from plea to praise. The most compelling hypothesis is that the turn is caused by a "salvation oracle" that is indeed caring and transformative. See Claus Westermann,

Praise and Lament in the Psalms (Atlanta: John Knox Press, 1981). Edgar W. Conrad, *Fear Not Warrior, BSJ* 75 (Chico, Calif.: Scholars Press, 1985) and Brueggemann, *Message of Psalms*, 56–58. The basic hypothesis is that of Hans Joachim Begrich, "Die priesterliche Tora," *ZAW* 52 (1934): 18–92, reprinted in *Gesammelte Studien zum Alten Testament, ThB.* 21 (Munich: Chr. Kaiser Verlag, 1964): 217–31.

26. Conrad, *Warrior*, chap. 5, has carefully analyzed the uses in Second Isaiah. He has shown that the "fear not" formula variously leads to assurance or to summons. Both, however, function in ways that are transformative.

27. On the formula as "exile-ending," see Walter Brueggemann, "Genesis L:15–21; a Theological Exploration," *VTSup* 36 (1983): 40–53.

28. On the phrase, see Martin E. Marty, *A Cry of Absence* (San Francisco: Harper and Row, 1983).

29. On the pathology of speech that precludes community, see Eugene Rosenstock Huessey, *The Origin of Speech* (Norwich, Vt.: Argo Books, 1981), chap. 2.

30. On the praise that emerges out of hurt processed, see Walter Brueggemann, *Israel's Praise*.

31. Westermann, *Praise and Lament*, 33, 73–75.

32. On the language of friendship as a way of speaking about God, see Sallie McFague, *Metaphorical Theology* (Philadelphia: Fortress Press, 1982), 177–92.

33. See Bernhard W. Anderson, "The Song of Miriam Poetically and Theologically Considered," *Directions in Biblical Hebrew Poetry*, ed. Elaine R. Follis, *JSOT Sup.* 40 (Sheffield, Wis.: Sheffield Academic Press, 1987): 285–96.

34. On the function of singing as an act of bold faith see Gail O'Day, "Singing Woman's Song: A Hermeneutic of Liberation," *CTM* 12 (1988): 203–10. O'Day specifically takes up the song of Miriam.

35. See Terence E. Fretheim, "Creation's Praise of God in the Psalms," *Ex Auditu* 3 (1987): 16–30.

36. On the overflow, see Daniel W. Hardy and David F. Ford, *Praising and Knowing God* (Philadelphia: Westminster Press, 1985), 109. They refer (142) to the "jazz factor" in which praise is irrepressible in response to God's overwhelming abundance.

37. On the Book of Revelation as a resource of preaching and a model for worship, see *Interpretation* 40.3 (1986), and the articles by Barr, Boring, and Craddock. Note especially Fred B. Craddock, "Preaching from the Book of Revelation," 270–82. Craddock writes (278): "Finally Revelation invites the reader to

sing, to pray, and to praise God. The book is primarily liturgical. Before planning a single sermon from this text, let the preacher read through Revelation in one or two sittings, marking every shout, every doxology, every prayer, every hallelujah, every benediction, every song. Clearly it was composed for use in the worship service of the church . . . "

38. On the Lord's Prayer as a prayer prayed out of the tradition of the Old Testament, see Paul van Buren, *A Theology of Jewish-Christian Reality*, 2 (San Francisco: Harper and Row, 1987), 288–94.

39. See Hardy and Ford, *Praising and Knowing God*, chap. 1 on "threats to praise."

40. On conversations as a method for theological work, see Paul van Buren, *A Theology of Jewish-Christian Reality 1* (San Francisco: Harper and Row, 1987), 27–44, and David Tracy, *The Analogical Imagination* (New York: Crossroad 1981), 446–55.

41. Moshe Greenberg, *Biblical Prose Prayer* (Berkeley and Los Angeles: University of California Press, 1983), chap. 1, has shown well that biblical prayer intends to impinge upon God in order to draw God back into a vital relation. This is done by way of lament in establishing common interest between God and the petitioner in the crisis of prayer.

3: RESTLESSNESS AND GREED

1. On "rearticulation" in recent scholarship, see Joseph W. Groves, *Actualization and Interpretation in the Old Testament*, (Atlanta: Scholars Press, 1987). See Claus Westermann, ed., *Essays on Old Testament Hermeneutics* (Richmond: John Knox Press, 1963) on which Groves bases much of his argument. Gerhard von Rad, in *Studies in Deuteronomy*, SBT 9 (Chicago: Henry Regnery Company, 1953) and in many other places has seen that much of Israel's law is interpreted, preached law.

2. On the foundational character of the commands, see Walter Brueggemann, "The Commandments and Liberated, Liberating Bonding," *Journal for Preachers* 10.2 (Lent, 1987): 15–24.

3. On the question of "goodness," see Mary Gordon, *Men and Angels* (New York: Random House, 1985), 200: "How I hate the word 'goodness.' What an obstacle it is to the moral life," said Jane. "Do you find goodness and morality incompatible?" Anne asked. "Of course not. But the term 'goodness' has been so perverted, so corrupted, it now covers only two or three virtues when there are hundreds."

4. On false notions of freedom generated by the Enlightenment, see Colin Gunton, *Enlightenment and Alienation* (Grand Rapids: Eerdmans Publishing Company, 1985). See especially Gunton's utilization of Iris Murdoch's *The Sovereignty of Good* (London: Methuen, 1985), and her notion of "obedience to creation." The argument of Gunton and Murdoch is that freedom is always dialectically related to obedience. It is the dialectic that must be recovered in the ethical reflection of the church.

5. On "listening," see Paul Ricoeur, *The Conflict of Interpretation* (Evanston: Northwestern University Press, 1974), 448–55. Ricoeur refers to hearing as "preethical obedience" (451).

6. Abraham Heschel, *Who Is Man?* (Stanford, Calif.: Stanford University Press, 1965), 97–98, 111–12.

7. See C. B. MacPherson, *The Political Theory of Possessive Individualism* (New York: Oxford University Press, 1962).

8. On the modern problem of fatigue, see Paul Tournier, ed., *Fatigue in Modern Society* (Richmond: John Knox Press, 1965).

9. On the one hand, Dorothy Solle, *Beyond Mere Obedience* (Minneapolis: Augsburg, 1970), has trenchantly critiqued the reduction of obedience to mere convention. Daniel Yankelovitch, *New Rules* (New York: Random House, 1981), on the other hand, has provided critique of the ideology of self-fulfillment that regards obedience as irrelevant and outmoded.

10. The Bible is able to imagine and narrate a situation in which there is not "too little" or "too much"; cf. Exod. 16:18, 2 Cor. 8:15.

11. Paul Ricoeur, "The Language of Faith," *The Philosophy of Paul Ricoeur,* ed. Charles E. Reagan and David Stewart (Boston: Beacon Press, 1978), 223–28. See also Ricoeur, "Toward a Hermeneutic of the Idea of Revelation," *Essays on Biblical Interpretation,* ed. Lewis Mudge (Philadelphia: Fortress Press, 1980), 117. On imagination as crucial for transformation, see Paul W. Pruyser, *The Play of Imagination* (New York: International Universities Press, Inc., 1983), esp. chap. 4.

12. Paul van Buren, *A Theology of the Jewish-Christian Reality 2* (San Francisco: Harper and Row, 1983), esp. 153–83, has demonstrated this common acknowledgment on the part of Jews and Christians. See also M. H. Goshen-Gottstein, "Tanakh Theology: The Religion of the Old Testament and Jewish Biblical Theology," *Ancient Israelite Religion,* ed. Patrick D. Miller Jr., et al., (Philadelphia: Fortress Press, 1987), 628–30.

13. See the programmatic essay of Emil Fackenheim, *To Mend the World* (New York: Schocken Books, 1982).

14. On the juxtaposition of ethics and imagination, see Stanley Hauerwas with Philip Foubert, "On Keeping Theological Ethics Imaginative," in *Against the Nations,* Stanley Hauerwas (Minneapolis: Winston Press, 1985), 54, 59. They write, "While we do not dispute the recognition that the moral life has a heavy stake in upholding normality, we wish to emphasize how profoundly 'the normal' requires and depends upon imagination . . . .Our imagination is the very means by which we live morally, and our moral life is in truth the source of our imagination."

15. On the relation between imagination and eschatology, see Amos Wilder, *Theopoetic: Theology and the Religious Imagination* (Philadelphia: Fortress Press, 1976), 95–100 and passim. The articulation of the end of the current disproportion, which is an eschatological conviction, can only be done by way of poetic imagination, for the anticipation runs well beyond our concrete experience.

16. On the necessity of interpretation and the fact that interpretation must always be done and must go in unexpected directions, see two very different statements, by David Tracy, *The Analogical Imagination* (New York: Crossroads, 1981), 115–24, 156–67, and Clark H. Pinnock, *The Scripture Principle* (San Francisco: Harper and Row, 1984), 197–221. See Brueggemann, "The Commandments and Liberated, Liberating Bonding," cited in n. 3.

17. On the cruciality and dynamic of the tradition of commandments, see Brevard S. Childs, *Old Testament Theology in a Canonical Context* (Philadelphia: Fortress Press, 1986), 63–83. See also his programmatic statement, 57–61, and his more general comments, 204–21.

18. On authority and interpretation, see Michael Fishbane, *Biblical Interpretation in Ancient Israel* (Oxford: Clarendon Press, 1985) with his attention to the interrelatedness of *traditum* and *tradition.*

19. On the Sabbath commandment, see Patrick D. Miller Jr., "The Human Sabbath: A Study in Deuteronomic Theology," *Princeton Seminary Bulletin* 6.2 (1985): 81–97.

20. A startling theological claim is made for the Sabbath as God's day of rest in Exod. 31:17: " . . . The Lord made heaven and earth, and on the seventh day he rested and was refreshed." The text uses the verb *naphash* in the reflexive, suggesting that Yahweh was exhausted, diminished, and the Sabbath made it possible for God to receive life back. This is an amazing affirmation both about the Sabbath and about God.

21. Hans Walter Wolff, *Anthropology of the Old Testament* (Philadelphia: Fortress Press, 1974), 139–40.

22. See H. Donner, "Jesaja lvi 1–7: ein Abrogationsfall innerhalb des Kanons—Implikationen und Konsequenzen," *VTSup* 36 (1983): 81–95, and Michael Fishbane, *Biblical Interpretations*, 257–62.

23. On these texts, see Luise Schottroff and Wolfgang Stegemann, "The Sabbath Was Made for Man," in *God of the Lowly*, ed. Willy Schottroff and Wolfgang Stegemann (Maryknoll, N.Y.: Orbis Books, 1984), 118–28.

24. On the cruciality and revolutionary potential of interpretation, see Michael Walzer, *Interpretation and Social Criticism* (Cambridge, Mass.: Harvard University Press, 1987). In the prophetic use (interpretation) of the Torah tradition, Walzer asserts: "Amos has won a kind of victory, the only kind that is available: he has evoked the core values of his audience in a powerful and plausible way" (89). Such an evocation is the work of preaching as an interpretation of the ethical tradition.

25. On "letting go" as an ethical posture, see Marie Augusta Neal, *A Socio-Theology of Letting Go* (New York: Paulist Press, 1977).

26. Northrup Frye, *The Critical Path* (Bloomington, Ind.: Indiana University Press, 1971), 171, writes, "The world of imagination from this point of view, is partly a holiday or Sabbath world where we rest from belief and commitment, the greater mystery beyond whatever can be formulated and presented for acceptance."

27. Marvin Cheney, "You Shall Not Covet Your Neighbor's House," *Pacific Theological Review* 15.2 (Winter, 1982): 3–13.

28. Greed is the invisible cause and underside of poverty. On the recognition that greed is not simply careless selfishness but is a systemic practice, see Bernhard Lang, "The Social Organisation of Peasant Poverty in Biblical Israel," *JSOT* 24 (1982): 47–63, and D. N. Premnoth, "Latifundialization and Isaiah 5:8–10," *JSOT* 40 (1988): 49–60.

29. See Norman K. Gottwald, *The Tribes of Yahweh* (Maryknoll, N.Y.: Orbis Books, 1979), 158–59, 266–67, 481–83 and passim, and Robert B. Coote, *Amos Among the Prophets* (Philadelphia: Fortress Press, 1981, 24–45. On the general theme of latifundialization, see D. N. Premnath, "The Process of Latifundialization Mirrored in the Oracles Pertaining to 8th Century BCE, in the Books of Amos, Hosea, Isaiah, and Micah," (Graduate Theological Union, 1984), and Andrew Dearman, *Property Rights in the Eighth-Century Prophets* (Atlanta: Scholars Press, 1988).

30. MacPherson, *The Political Theory of Possessive Individualism*, 24, summarizes Hobbes' view of conflict in society: "In short, the matter about which competition and difference would lead to a war of each with all, is the civilized matter of cultivated land and 'convenient seats'." It is indeed land, and being able to "plant, sow, build, or possess a convenient seat" that characterizes social reality. It is important that on this point, Hobbes anticipates Marx. It is more important for the preacher that Israel had understood long before any modern social philosopher that God's will concerns land, and that land constitutes the key dimension of social possibility and social conflict.

31. See also Hans Walter Wolff, "Micah the Moreshite—The Prophet and His Background," in *Israelite Wisdom*, ed. John G. Gammie (Missoula, Mont.: Scholars Press, 1978), 77–84.

32. This is a parade example for the thesis of Patrick D. Miller Jr., *Sin and Judgment in the Prophets* (Chico, Calif.: Scholars Press, 1982), 29–31, that prophetic punishment is closely paralleled to the sin asserted.

33. On the cruciality of the "urban elite" in ancient Israel and on the complexity of the critical problems with the data, see most recently Robert B. Coate and Keith W. Whitelam, *The Emergence of Early Israel in Historical Perspective* (Sheffield, England: Almond Press, 1987).

34. The notion that land grabbing leads to death is affirmed both from the claims of revelation and from the process of historical experience. The juxtaposition of revelation and experience in this particular case supports the thesis of Erhard Gerstenberger, *Wesen and Herkunft des "Apodiktischen Rechts,"* WMANT 20 (Neukirchen-Vluyn: Neukirchener Verlag, 1965) that the commandments have their source in the instruction and experience of the tribe. The teachings that are essential to survival and well-being in the tribe come to be authorized as the commandments of God. Walter Harrelson, *The Ten Commandments and Human Rights, OBT* (Philadelphia: Fortress Press, 1980), 152, makes explicit reference to the public, international dimension of coveting and death.

35. On the common vocabulary of forgiveness and debt cancellation, see Douglas E. Oakman, "Jesus and Agrarian Palestine: The Factor of Debt," *Society of Biblical Literature, 1985 Seminar Papers* (Atlanta: Scholars Press, 1985), 57–73.

36. On the social significance of the Jubilee practice see John Howard Yoder, *The Politics of Jesus* (Grand Rapids: Eerdmans Publishing Company, 1972), 64–77, and Neale, *Letting Go*, 5–8. For a working definition of "justice," I have proposed

the following, "Voices in the Night—Against Justice," *To Act Justly, Love Tenderly, Walk Humbly,* Walter Brueggemann et al., (New York: Paulist Press, 1986), 5: "Justice is to work out what belongs to whom, and to return it to them." The practice of the Jubilee year that assumes social entitlement is a paradigmatic practice of such justice.

37. On this critical understanding of Third Isaiah, see Paul D. Hanson, *The Dawn of Apocalyptic* (Philadelphia: Fortress Press, 1975), 59–77, and Elizabeth Achtemeier, *The Community and Message of Isaiah 56–66* (Minneapolis: Augsburg, 1982), 86–94.

38. More generally on the social significance of prison and bondage, see Michel Foucault, *Discipline and Punishment: The Birth of the Prison* (New York: Pantheon Books, 1977).

39. For concrete examples in the Bible of the continuing force of this legal tradition, see Jeremiah 34 and Nehemiah 5.

40. See Michael Crosby, *The Spirituality of the Beatitudes* (Maryknoll, N.Y.: Orbis Books, 1981), and *Thy Will Be Done* (Maryknoll, N.Y.: Orbis Books, 1977), and Sharon Ringe, *Jesus, Liberation and the Biblical Jubilee* (Philadelphia: Fortress Press, 1985). Patrick D. Miller Jr., "Luke 4:16–21," *Interpretation* 29 (1975): 417–21, has well explicated the dimension of debt cancellation in the gospel use of this text. He pays particular attention to the verb *aphesis,* which is frequently misunderstood and reduced in our common rendering of "release." Helpful resources in this regard may be found in *Social Themes of the Christian Year: A Commentary on the Lectionary,* ed. Dieter T. Hessel (Philadelphia: The Geneva Press, 1983) and *Preaching as a Social Act: Theory and Practice,* ed. Arthur van Seters (Nashville: Abingdon Press, 1988).

41. On resting life in God's hand, see Matitiahu Tsevat, "The Basic Meaning of the Biblical Sabbath," *The Meaning of the Book of Job and Other Biblical Studies* (New York: Ktav, 1980), 48, who characterizes the Sabbath this way: "Every seventh day the Israelite renounces his autonomy and affirms God's dominion over him." See also W. Gunther Plaut, "The Sabbath as Protest: Thoughts on Work and Leisure in the Automated Society," *Tradition and Change in Jewish Experience,* ed. A. L. Johnson, 169–83.

42. On the relation between serious morality and serious literary art, see the exquisite statement by Robert Stone, "The Reason for Stories: Toward a Moral Fiction," *Harper's Magazine* 276, June, 1988, 71–76.

43. On the pastoral use of imagination, see the suggestive comments of Jack L. Seymour, Robert T. O'Gorman, and Charles R. Foster, *The Church in the Education of the Public* (Nashville:

Abingdon Press, 1984), 134–56. Their reference to "sacramental imagination" is congruent with my argument here. They deal with the matter of education, I with preaching, but both discussions are concerned with the *public* reality of the church. Imagination is crucial, either in education or preaching, that the church may think and act faithfully in its public life. They assert, "the imagination of a people is stunted by the influence of an acquisitive, competitive, materialistic society . . . Such stunting blocks a culture's spiritual potential and creates a religionless public. We as church educators must respond to this void" (135). That is correct, except that a fullness of idolatry may be even worse than a void. More directly related to our subject, see Philip S. Keane, *Christian Ethics and Imagination* (New York: Paulist Press, 1984).

44. Isak Dinesen, "Babette's Feast," *Babette's Feast and Other Anecdotes of Destiny* (Vintage Books; New York: Random House, 1988), 3–48, has provided a wondrous interpretive exposition of the power of feast, and likely of the power of the Eucharist.

4: RESISTANCE AND RELINQUISHMENT

1. John Calvin, *Institute of Christian Religion Book One, Chapter 1*, ed. John T. McNeill, *LCC* 20 (Philadelphia: Westminster Press, 1973): 33–39, understood well the interrelatedness of God and human persons, and furthermore that the latter derives from the former.

2. On the brutality of depersonalization and the capacity to counter such brutality, see Elaine Scarry, *The Body in Pain* (New York: Oxford University Press, 1985).

3. See John J. Collins, "The Place of Apocalypticism in the Religion of Israel," *Ancient Israelite Religion*, ed. Patrick D. Miller et. al. (Philadelphia: Fortress Press, 1987), 539–58, and his references to the work of Hanson. Collins, "Daniel and His Social World," *Interpretation* 39 (1985): 143, speaks of the cruciality of "illusions."

4. John J. Collins, "Daniel and His Social World," 135, can assert, "There is no urgency in the tales. It is sufficient that the God of Israel is ultimately in control." On the contemporary practice of such confidence, see Beatriz Melano Couch, "Confidence in God at the End of the Twentieth Century," *The Princeton Seminary Bulletin* 9 (1988): 1–7. The confidence urged by Couch is against the data, exactly the same urging made in the Daniel narratives.

5. See W. Sibley Towner, "Daniel 1 in the Context of the Canon," in *Canon, Theology, and Old Testament Interpretation*, ed. Gene M. Tucker, et al. (Philadelphia: Fortress Press, 1988), 285–98, and Joyce G. Baldwin, *Daniel*, Tyndale Old Testament Commentaries (Madison, Wis.: Inter-Varsity Press, 1978), 82–83.

6. See the splendid essay of Lynne Shawn Schwartz, "Daniel," and Mark Mirsky, "Daniel," in *Congregation*, ed. David Rosenberg (London: Harcourt, Brace, Jovanovich, 1987), 418–34, 435–55. Schwarts (433) concludes: "Daniel, in exile, dreamed dreams of regaining his true life, if he would only hold fast to the truth. He told those around him their lost dreams and their life stories. He had to go into a dark, savage place, and came out unhurt, telling no one of what he felt or did there. He read the writing on the wall and saw what it meant and told it. Above all, like most dreamers, he performed his necessary, difficult work, he waited, trusting God's words, 'Blessed is he that waiteth'" (12:12).

In parallel fashion, Mirsky offers a powerful conclusion (454): "And what do we know of death but such dreams? It is for this reason that the voice of the angel in the book of Daniel has such authority for us. It seems to speak out of the soft assurance of a parent, my mother bending over the bed, singing in her lovely, throaty voice, / Close your eyes,/ And you'll have a surprise./ The sandman is coming./ He's coming, he's coming. It is the voice which urges one down into sleep in the hope not of extinction but of joy. To hear that voice one second after death would redeem all earthly pain."

7. Babylon is clearly not to be taken historically, but is a cipher for any and every oppression, and Nebuchadnezzar is a sub-set of Babylon as a cipher that can refer to every current oppressor. The loosening of the references to Babylon and Nebuchadnezzar from their historical locus serves the canonical reinterpretation of the narratives. On the reuse of the metaphors, see William Stringfellow, *An Ethic for Christians and Other Aliens in a Strong Land* (Waco, Tex.: Word Books, 1973) on the Book of Revelation. See esp. chaps. 1 and 4.

8. See Jeremiah 25:9; 27:6.

9. Bruno Bettelheim, *Surviving the Holocaust* (London: Penguin Books, 1986) has recounted the modest but decisive ways in which he maintained his own freedom even in a death camp. The maintenance of freedom may seem "objectively" unimportant, but it is, as Bettelheim attests, crucial for the survival of hope and sanity.

10. W. Sibley Towner, *Daniel,* Interpretation (Atlanta: John Knox Press, 1984), 26–27, notes the connections of the Daniel narratives and the poetry of Isaiah 40–55. See John Gammie, "On the Intention and Sources of Daniel i–vi," *VT* 31(1981):282–92.

11. "Fatness" (*dsn*) is a sign of well-being, blessedness, and prosperity; our contemporary "eating disorders" were not absent in that ancient, demanding society.

12. Richard J. Clifford, "Isaiah 55: Invitation of a Feast," in *The Word of the Lord Shall Go Forth,* ed. Carol L. Meyers and M. O'Connor (Winona Lake, Ind.: Eisenbrauns, 1983), 27–35, has suggested that the call of Isaiah 55:1–3 has its antecedents in the "call of wisdom." If this is so, then the summons to "live" is not unlike the summons of wisdom in Prov. 8:35–36.

13. Collins, "Daniel and His Social World," is clear that the Daniel narratives are important "acts of imagination," but they voice no specific criticism of established power and recommend no specific action. In that sense, they are contrasted with the urgency of the Maccabean movement and rhetoric that is aimed at concrete action.

14. See Donald E. Gowan, *When Man Becomes God* (Pittsburgh: Pickwick Press, 1975), 121–28.

15. W. Lee Humphreys, "A Life-Style for Diaspora: A Study of the Tales of Esther and Daniel," *JBL* 92 (1973): 221, has noted that the narrative does not focus on the character of the king, but on the role and function of the courtiers.

16. In my discussion I will follow the verse numbers of the English translations.

17. See Sibley W. Towner, "The Poetic Passages of Daniel 1–6" *CBQ* 31 (1969): 317–26.

18. On the social power and importance of doxology, see Walter Brueggemann, *Israel's Praise.*

19. While the characterizations of Daniel in chap. 1 and chap. 4 are clearly distinct, the narrative effect is cumulative. In the present form of the literature, the fact that Daniel resisted the empire in chap. 1 gives Daniel freedom and authority in Daniel 4. See below on the narrative interface of Nebuchadnezzar and Daniel in these two narratives.

20. On the contemporary crisis of such an epistemological break, see Sharon D. Welch, *Communities of Resistance and Solidarity* (Maryknoll, N.Y.: Orbis Books, 1985).

21. This epistemological break is precisely articulated by Paul in 1 Cor. 1:25. The Daniel narrative engages in just such a dangerous inversion of reality.

22. See Andre Lacocque, *The Book of Daniel* (Atlanta: John Knox Press, 1979), 77–81.

23. The role of Daniel in addressing Nebuchadnezzar is not unlike that of Nathan in speaking to David in 2 Sam. 12:7. Nathan says, *'attāh hā 'iš*; Daniel says, *'anth-hû*. The presenting of the problem in both cases is through "illusion," i.e., a parable and a dream.

24. The transformation is not unlike the "renewal of your mind" in Rom. 12:2.

25. Obedience as the proper mode for right faith and right understanding is affirmed by both Calvin and Heschel. Calvin, *Institutes*, 72 concludes: "But not only faith, perfect and in every way complete, but all right knowledge of God is born of obedience . . . ." Abraham Heschel, *Who Is Man?* (Stanford, Calif.: Stanford University Press, 1965), 111, from a very different perspective asserts, "I am commanded—therefore I am."

26. See the eloquent summary of Towner, *Daniel*, 67–68.

27. On the gift of new life "from above," see Gail R. O'Day, *The Word Disclosed* (St. Louis: CBP Press, 1987), 16–28, and "New Birth as a New People: Spirituality and Community in the Fourth Gospel," *Word and World* 8.1 (1988): 53–61.

28. On the emergence of such autonomy see Alasdair MacIntyre, *After Virtue* (Notre Dame, Ind.: University of Notre Dame Press, 1981), and Bellah, *Habits of the Heart*. In his more recent study, *Whose Justice? Which Rationality?* (Notre Dame, Ind.: University of Notre Dame Press, 1988), esp. 326–48, MacIntyre has shown that even the notion of autonomy is in fact the product of an historical tradition that has its own warrants and makes its own requirements, and is therefore subject to criticism. Thus the tradition of autonomy is not in fact "autonomous," as it appears and claims to be.

29. This is the argument of Gowan, *When Man Becomes God*. In the texts studied by Gowan, it may be affirmed that God has given all things, but in fact the arrogant human agent proceeds as though God had given nothing, and that the human agent is self-made and indebted to none.

30. On the adequacy of the word of the gospel in the most troubled situations, Joseph Sittler, *Gravity and Grace* (Minneapolis: Augsburg, 1986), 63, has written: "In a sense, that's what a sermon is for: to hang the holy possible in front of the mind of the listeners and lead them to that wonderful moment when they say, 'If it were true, it would do.' To pass from that to belief is the work of the Holy Spirit, not of the preacher or the teacher."

Scripture Index

G

Wa
lifetin
At
texts
tweei
ancie
of Jer
"I
tion
and
man
gree
tradi